James Christie (1829–1892) was a graduate of Glasgow University and an ordained nonconformist minister who had changed tack and become a doctor. He would become physician to the Sultan of Zanzibar. He would get to know both Livingstone and Stanley and play a controversial part in the campaign to end the slave trade. He would marry, would nearly die of fever, and would fight to try to save the lives of countless cholera victims.

Finding himself in the thick of Zanzibar' worst cholera epidemic, his curiosity was the key to an amazing piece of medical detection which was the supreme achievement of his life and which deserves to be remembered today. His broadly based environmental and social concerns set him apart from the narrowly focused epidemiologists of the late nineteenth century.

On his return to Scotland, through his writings and his powerful pleas for reform, he also made a significant contribution to Scottish public health.

Edna Robertson has written a powerful biography of a nineteenth century medical pioneer. Using family papers including James Christie's letters to his brother Andrew in Kilmarnock and other sources, she does not shirk from the realities of Zanzibar before public sanitation nor from the horrors of the slave trade.

Christie of Zanzibar

Medical Pathfinder

Edna Robertson

for Khursheed Moos
with warm wishes
from
Edna

ARGYLL ✚ PUBLISHING

First published by
Argyll Publishing
Glendaruel
Argyll PA22 3AE
Scotland
www.argyllpublishing.com

British Library Cataloguing-in-Publication Data.
A catalogue record for this book in available from the British Library.

ISBN 978 1 906134 60 0

Printing: Bell & Bain Ltd, Glasgow

For Linda and Roger

Contents

Pic 1 James Christie, aged 36, just before his departure for Zanzibar in 1865.
This digital version of his photograph, which was preserved along with his letters in Cambridge University Archives, has been made available by Cambridge University Imaging Services department.

Pic 2 Christie in his Hillhead years.
(The David Livingstone Centre, Blantyre, the National Trust for Scotland)

Pic 3 Zanzibar waterfront including the Sultan's palace, with its blood-red flag fluttering in the breeze. (Zanzibar State Archives)

Pic 4 The old nineteenth-century British Consulate, with the U.S. Consulate next door. (Zanzibar State Archives)

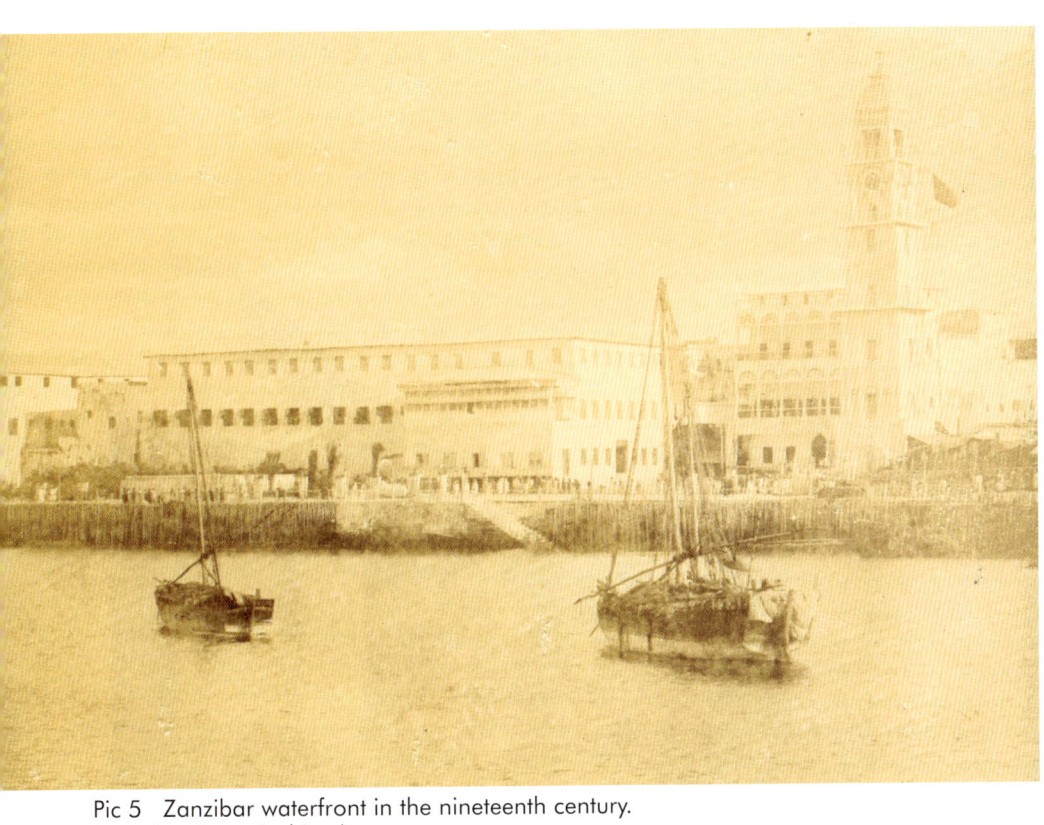

Pic 5   Zanzibar waterfront in the nineteenth century.
(Zanzibar State Archives)

Pic 6 Zanzibar town's maze of narrow, twisted streets still remains
(minus the smells.) (Zanzibar State Archives)

Pic 7 Dhow off Zanzibar.
(Zanzibar State Archives)

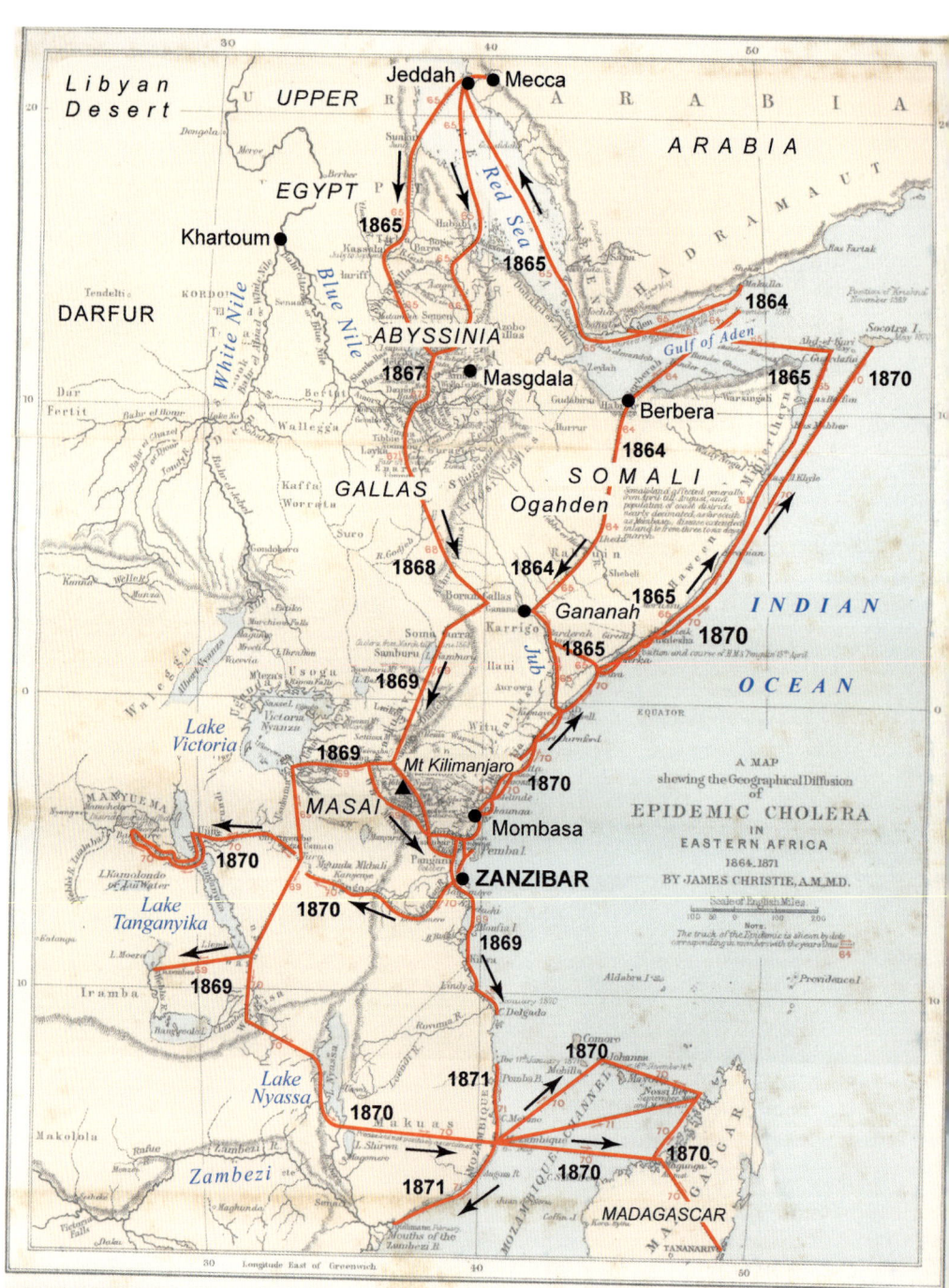

Pic 8 The cholera routes to Zanzibar. Map by Mike Shand, Glasgow University cartographer, modified from the maps in Christie's book.

Pic 9 British naval boarding party attempting to suppress the illegal slave trade. (Zanzibar State Archives)

Pic 10. Hillhead in Christie's day – the Opening Ceremony for the new Kelvin Bridge in 1891. But Hillhead's days as an independent burgh were ending. (Mitchell Library)

Pic 11 James Burn Russell, Medical Officer of Health for Glasgow from 1872 to 1898, who was a close friend of Christie's. The two conferred together almost daily.

Pic 12 John Service, a fellow student and lifelong friend of Christie's. Service later became minister of Hyndland Parish Church, Glasgow. The caricature is from the popular monthly magazine of the day, The Bailie.

This book was written with generous financial support from the Strathmartine Trust. I also wish to acknowledge generous help from the Guthrie Trust. Research grants from these two bodies enabled me to spend time working in Zanzibar State Archives and to follow the trail of James Christie's activities there.

I owe special thanks to the Centre for the History of Medicine at Glasgow University, with which I have a long-standing and, to me, much valued association. Several members of the centre supplied useful information derived from their own researches but in particular I wish to acknowledge the help and encouragement given to me by the centre's director, Professor Malcolm Nicolson, and by Professor Marguerite Dupree and Professor Lawrence Weaver, who scrutinised the typescript and made useful suggestions and criticisms.

The excellent library of the Royal College of Physicians and Surgeons of Glasgow proved an invaluable resource, and special thanks are due to Carol Parry, Library and Heritage Manager, and Valerie McClure, Assistant Librarian, for their unfailing willingness to provide expert help. Christie's book on cholera epidemics was almost unavailable during most of the time when I was working on his biography (a photographic reprint was only recently issued in the U.S.A.) and my task would have been impossible if I had not been given access to the college's volume, one of only two in Scotland.

Cambridge Uiversity Library was a key resource, in particular its archives, which contain the only copies of Christie's letters from Zanzibar, and its Imaging Services Department.

I am grateful to two friends who read the typescript – Sheriff Iain Macmillan, who made many useful suggestions and also helped with my research into Christie's Kilmarnock connection, and not least my former *Herald* colleague Lesley Duncan.

Thanks also to Muriel Murdoch, who took the opportunity during a stay in Angus to investigate the family background and local connections of Christie's wife, Betsy Kidd.

My thanks also to Dr Alistair Tough, NHS Greater Glasgow and Clyde Archivist, not only for help in researching hospital histories connected with Christie but also for his specialised knowledge of African medical history and the sustained interest he has taken in my research.

Anne Geddes, Heritage Services Librarian for East Ayrshire Council, and her colleagues at the Dick Institute in Kilmarnock including Archie Connell, produced valuable information about the Kilmarnock end of the story.

Karen Carruthers, of the David Livingstone Centre, Blantyre, National Trust for Scotland, made a studio portrait of Christie in his mature years available for reproduction. David Weir, local studies librarian at Paisley Central Library, kindly investigated Christie's failed application to become Medical Officer of Health for Renfrewshire.

Help was also received from Glasgow City Archives, the Glasgow Room of the Mitchell Library, Glasgow University Library, Glasgow University Archives and the Wellcome Institute Library, London. The staff of Zanzibar State Archives, where I spent a number of weeks, also deserve my thanks, as do others with whom I had useful discussions during my stay on the island, notably the historian Professor Abdul Sheriff and Bishop John Ramadhani. And thanks to Mshamara Chum Kombo, of Mahonda, Zanzibar, for great help in tracing Christie's footsteps on the island (and for introducing me to the delights of coconut water, straight from a tree in his garden).

Others to whom I owe thanks include Jeanne Brady, Dr Anna Crozier, Professor Myron Echenberg, Roger Webber, Yoland Brown, Dr Iain Smith, Mark Skippen, Dr David Sutton, Dr Elma Douglas, Colin Archard and Linda Chapman. My thanks also to Dr Ivy Barclay, with whom I corresponded on matters relating to Christie's membership of the Evangelical Union.

I am grateful to Mike Shand, of Glasgow University, for digital maps of the cholera routes, and to Jean Reid for doing the index.

Edna Robertson
August 2010

Preface

JAMES CHRISTIE reached Zanzibar late in November, 1865. The voyage from Gourock had taken three months and he was glad to see his destination at last. Only 25 miles from the East African mainland, the island had a tropical appearance, with its tall coconut trees fringing dazzling white sands, and Christie liked the look of the town where he was to live, its waterfront lined by whitewashed Arab houses and an ornate sultan's palace. But his nine years in Zanzibar were to be no idyll.

He was 36 years old, a graduate of Glasgow University and an ordained nonconformist minister who had changed tack and become a doctor, working in a mental asylum for two years before his departure for Zanzibar. His activities there were to be startlingly diverse. He had gone to Zanzibar as honorary physician to a Church of England mission but was to end his nine years there as physician to the Sultan of Zanzibar. He would get to know both Livingstone and Stanley and play a controversial part in the campaign to end the slave trade on the island. He would marry, would nearly die of fever, and would fight to try to save the lives of countless cholera victims. He would even display some short-lived entrepreneurial ambition and have a spell in charge of a sugar factory.

A man of restless energy, he once thought about becoming an explorer himself, envisaging a trek from Mombasa into unmapped Masai territory. He never made the journey but his curiosity about this area was the key to an amazing piece of medical detection which was the supreme achievement of his life and which deserves to be remembered today.

This episode began in 1869 when Christie found himself in the thick of Zanzibar's worst cholera epidemic, never allowing himself more than two hours' consecutive rest. Afterwards he set himself the task of analysing the reasons why the epidemic had wiped out the island's Africans and Arabs in their thousands but had hardly touched Hindus and resident Europeans, finding that ethnic customs provided the key to the explanation. He followed this up with a more ambitious investigation into the origins of the epidemic and the three previous ones, drawing on ethnology, meteorology and geography, politely pestering European traders for information, buttonholing expedition leaders and missionaries who had been on the mainland and 'strangers who happened to be in the place', studying the writings of the great explorers and the records in the British consulate and, above all, interviewing tribal leaders in Swahili – he emphatically didn't share the common view that native testimony was unreliable.

By patiently piecing together countless fragments of information he was able to prove that the epidemics had spread from Arabia (ultimately from India) along the great trade and pilgrim routes, both land and sea – and, crucially, that they had spread at the pace of human travel. This was a blow to those doctors who had continued to believe that the disease was spread by miasma and not by contaminated water and who were unconvinced by John Snow's famous investigations at the Broad Street pump two decades earlier.

The book that Christie wrote on cholera epidemics in East Africa[1] caused a stir in the medical world of the 1870s but was soon forgotten amid developments in bacteriology and parasitology. In the 1950s an East African pathologist, J.N.P. Davies, wrote a paper about its historical value as the earliest English-language medical treatise on East Africa and as a remarkable portrayal of the region at a time when Livingstone's explorations had aroused popular curiosity.[2] Yet Christie's work continued to be ignored in the west – in Glasgow he is remembered, if at all, for his book on the city's medical institutions – and he failed to gain the recognition that he dserved as an epidemiologist of stature, worthy to be ranked not far behind the great John Snow. The recent issue of a photographic reprint of Christie's book by an American publisher[3] should allow him to gain wider currency, and at the same time the full significance of his work has been recognised in a recent work by Christopher Hamlin, who gives Christie credit for spotting the importance of cultural differences in the spread of cholera and for identifying hygiene as an area of cultural expression.[4] His broadly based environmental and social concerns set him apart from the narrowly focused epidemiologists of the late nineteenth century and gave him an affinity with the eighteenth and twentieth centuries, not least in his interest in the role of climate in spreading cholera. He may be best seen as standing in the tradition of Professor William Pulteney Alison and other early nineteenth Scottish doctors who rejected the prevailing orthodoxy by insisting on the role of destitution in the spread of disease. Some historians believe that Alison, who was deeply influenced by the values of the Scottish Enlightenment, held out the possibility of a more humane and effective public health policy than the narrow, filth-centered sanitarianism of Edwin Chadwick. It may be significant that as a student at Glasgow University Christie was awarded prizes by Professor Andrew Buchanan, whose views were similar to Alison's.

The recent resurgence of epidemic cholera in Africa gives additional significance to Christie's work, which was a forerunner of modern cholera studies. With its unusual emphasis on the social dynamic revealed by responses to the disease it exemplifies what the historian Charles Rosenberg meant when he described cholera studies as a sampling device that can reveal much about a society.

I first came across Christie through an interest in Scottish public health history rather than through any expertise on Africa. For two months in 1880 he was acting medical officer of health for Glasgow during the illness of James Burn Russell, MOH, whose life I was researching. When I looked him up in the *Medical Directory* I saw that he was medical officer for the burgh of Hillhead, and also that he had been the Sultan of Zanzibar's doctor – an unusual career combination which made me want to know more.

This proved daunting. Christie left no descendants and no private papers. But one goldmine turned up in Cambridge University Archives – a large collection of long and quirky letters written by Christie in Zanzibar to his brother Andrew, a Kilmarnock ironmonger. As well as illuminating his life on the island they reveal some sides of his personality which would not otherwise be suspected. Faded photographs have been preserved along with the letters, and a family memoir written by his brother is in the Dick Institute in Kilmarnock (which also has on display a lion's head which he sent back from Zanzibar). I learned more on a recent trip to Zanzibar, where Christie is better remembered than he is here.

From these sources a picture emerges of a questing, unpredictable, sometimes impatient and testy man. He was 'of middle height, exact in dress, quiet in gait' and 'somewhat dignified', a restrained man, speaking calmly in a low voice in short, emphatic sentences. But one of his close friends noted that although he was restrained in manner he could be stirred into 'spurts of utterances' by anything he considered to be humbug. This is certainly true of his letters, in which he worked himself into a fury over, for example, what he saw as the hypocrisy of Queen Victoria. He accused her of 'humbug and cant' because, even in the midst of mourning Prince Albert, she had contemplated – so Christie had heard – depriving another woman of a husband by marrying one of her daughters to a 'German adventurer' who already had a wife. A more serious target of his outrage was the British Government's policy of attempting to check the slave trade by boarding slave boats; a better approach, he argued, would be to open up other forms of trade and offer compensation to the sultan for closing the slave market. Christie's 'spurts of utterances' were also frequently provoked by the British consul, John Kirk, who was later to become virtual ruler of Zanzibar.

In argument Christie was 'lance-like and unrelenting' with a 'clear cold style'. But his friends also found him kindly and genial in a humorous and unfussy way. One of his closest friends, James Burn Russell, wrote after his death:

> It will be long before I cease to see Christie as he used to
> enter my room – right hand usually in his trouser pocket,
> from which he did not withdraw it until he had made a
> slight ceremonious bow, with an apologetic 'don't let me
> interrupt you,' spoken like an aside. Rarely did a week pass
> without such a visit and a short chat on something
> concerning the subject uppermost in both our minds.

Christie led a quiet life on his return to Glasgow, becoming a professor at Anderson's Medical College and Medical Officer of Health for the burgh of Hillhead before it became swallowed up by Glasgow. But he continued to write papers on tropical medicine as well as on other subjects. His voluminous output covered subjects ranging from yellow fever in the US to sanitation in small Scottish towns, from suicide to exotic tropical skin diseases. Through his writings and his powerful pleas for reform he also made a significant contribution to Scottish public health.

One of his colleagues once wrote that although Christie was a successful medical practitioner he would have been more successful if he had spent less time writing. But it was the restless curiosity behind his writings that was the key to his life's great work, his cholera book. He was frustrated in his wish to become an explorer but perhaps his adventures in epidemiology allowed him to achieve his ambition at one remove.

CHAPTER 1

Strathaven Days

JAMES CHRISTIE seems at first glance an unlikely man to have become physician to the Sultan of Zanzibar. He was a Lanarkshire lad, born in the weaving town of Strathaven to parents of modest means. There was nothing flamboyant about his personality – he was precise in manner and some people considered him a trifle prim.

Yet there was a hint of adventure in his family background. His father, also called James Christie, was a Caithness man, a farmer's son who was not attracted to a settled life. When he was 20, in 1793, he and his brother had been among the men of Caithness who enlisted in the Breadalbane Fencibles during the recruitment drive that had followed the French Revolution. For an extra bounty of two guineas he later volunteered to help suppress Wolfe Tone's rebellion in Ireland. In later life he was reluctant to speak of the horrors that he had seen there. His brother remained in the army and fell fighting the French in Madras but James Christie senior took his discharge in 1802 and worked in Paisley for a while before moving to Strathaven, in the Lanarkshire parish of Avondale. He set up in business as a cloth merchant, opening a small shop in the town and travelling on his pony around Fenwick Moor with his wares. It sounds a humble occupation, but he managed to have his portrait painted in oils, wearing a tartan cloak with a crimson hood and displaying, in the words of one of his descendants, 'a delicate, sensitive mouth and a fine Wellingtonian nose'.[1]

At the age of 53 he married a local woman 20 years younger than himself. Mary Fleming was one of 10 children in a local farming family, and one of a large number of Flemings in Avondale parish. James, who was born about three years later, on May 12, 1829, was the middle child of three. His sister Elizabeth was two years older and his brother Andrew, to whom James was to remain closely attached all his life, was two-and-a-half years younger, having been born when their mother was 41.

The Christie children did not have a particularly strict upbringing, certainly as far as their father was concerned. His soft and melodious Highland voice was seldom raised in anger and he was very patient with children. 'Any scolding the children may have required was supplied by their mother,' wrote James Christie's nephew – the son of his brother Andrew – in a privately published memoir a century later.[2] James inherited his mother's 'reserved and precise' demeanour and his father's gentle manner, though not his rather stout physique.

The three Christie children had plenty to interest them in the Strathaven of the 1830s, with its ruined medieval castle standing above the narrow and irregular streets of the old burgh. The place was thriving – the population had doubled to 3000 in the two decades before James's birth; there were bustling weekly markets and annual fairs. Social and rustic festivities, in the words of the local minister, writing six years after Christie's birth, helped to relieve the monotony of the long winter evenings. In addition, there were excellent inns, probably not frequented by the Christies, and the local diet included butcher meat which was said to be 'only little (if at all) inferior to that of Glasgow'. Dairy produce, including first-class Dunlop cheese – for which Christie was to develop such a taste that he asked for some to be sent to him in Zanzibar – was brought to the Strathaven market from the surrounding countryside, where huge tracts of lands had been reclaimed and new drainage schemes were in progress everywhere.

By the time of James's birth most of Strathaven's houses and all its shops were lit by gas and new villas had been built by the wealthier citizens. Many of the town's 800 or so weavers owned their own homes.

Communications had opened up – there were coaches to Glasgow, Edinburgh and Ayr every day except Sunday, as well countless post-horses and chaises and gigs.[3] The young Christie brothers were among local boys who used to gather to watch the stagecoach on its way between Edinburgh and Ayr.

Latin, Greek, English, grammar, writing and arithmetic were taught in the village school, which was just along the road from the Christies' house in Kirk Street in the heart of the village. Almost every child over the age of six was able to read and the local minister claimed in 1835 that 'many good scholars have been taught here.' Christie's nephew later recounted in his family memoir that in winter the pupils took turns to provide fuel to keep the schoolroom fire burning brightly. He also noted that although education was free to the poor the dominie was very severe on the poorly clad Irish children whose parents had come to Strathaven to build the new roads and railways.

Even for the more prosperous, life was not always a pastoral idyll. The cholera pandemic which had reached Glasgow in 1832 arrived in Strathaven three years later, when Christie was six. His earliest memories, as he was to write in later life, were of this epidemic, in which some 50 people died.[4] Forty years on, he would return to his home town and in a lecture describe the foul state of the town's sanitation at the time of the cholera epidemic, adding that it was still dreadful.

The Christies escaped cholera but trouble was fast approaching. In 1839, when James was 10, his father died at the age of 66. During his lengthy illness he had been unable to attend to his work with the result that when his affairs were settled the family was left with one shilling. It seems unlikely that in the hungry forties all their debtors paid up, although Mrs Christie appears to have kept the business going for a little while at least for she was described as a merchant in the 1841 census.

Another worry was James's younger brother. Andrew was a delicate lad and when he was about 10 he was sent for the good of his health to work as a herdsman on a nearby farm. In later years he attributed his robust constitution to these six weeks of outdoor labour, but the remuneration was not great. He had been promised a shilling but was given sixpence, not a huge contribution to the family finances.[5]

But soon the family began to break up. In 1846 James's sister Elizabeth, then 19, married and in the same year Andrew Christie, approaching 14, left home to become an errand boy in a toolmaker's shop in Glasgow with the promise of an apprenticeship after a year. The country lad evidently revelled in city life, attending lectures by Thackeray and Kossuth and readings by Dickens as well as hearing the best opera singers of the day.

The more scholarly James was to have a more formal education but not until several years after his schooldays. The gap years between school and university are not well documented but Christie was still in Strathaven at the age of 19, presumably working to help support his widowed mother and save for his university education. It was then, in 1848, that another cholera epidemic reached the town, resulting in many sudden deaths. More than 20 years later Christie would recall these scenes while cholera victims were dropping dead in the streets of Zanzibar. But for the moment he had no plans to become a doctor.

CHAPTER *2*
Apprentice Evangelist

JAMES CHRISTIE'S first serious ambition was to be a preacher. When he was 21 he finally went to Glasgow University to study arts and at the same time enrolled as a student in the theological academy of the Evangelical Union, whose classes were held during the university vacation.

It was a brave choice, given the state of the family's finances. The Evangelical Union, still in its infancy when he embarked on his theological studies, was not a wealthy organisation. Its ministers were paid only about £60 a year, considerably less than a doctor would earn at the outset of his career. It offered no financial help to its students when Christie began his studies although in his final year he was awarded one of the three main EU bursaries on offer. The classes took up all of August and September, leaving less time for remunerative vacation jobs especially since a huge amount of reading was required. And its students tended to be shunned by members of other presbyterian churches because of their unorthodox doctrines.[1]

So what made Christie opt for such an unremunerative and socially isolated career? He had grown up in Covenanting country which nurtured many religious nonconformists (David Livingstone among them). Only a few miles from Strathaven was Drumclog, where in the 'Killing Times' of the late seventeeth century a strategically placed group of local Covenanters had won a famous victory over government troops under Graham of Claverhouse. No doubt the young Christie's imagination was stirred by such tales as he walked on the lonely moorland where the Covenanters had once gathered to hear their ministers preach sermons full of divine wrath and judgements to come. When he was in his teens such scenes were re-enacted when members of the Evangelical Union, gaining adherents more rapidly than they could build churches, carried their message to the countryside around Strathaven. As one observer noted, 'the scream of the lapwing and the plaintive cry of the curlew and the plover seemed to give additional solemnity to the scene' [2] as the sermon began with the 59th Paraphrase:

> Behold what witnesses unseen
> Encompass us around . . .

But Christie was not stepping in the footsteps of the Covenanters when he threw in his lot with the Evangelical Union. Its services had a more revivalist flavour, the sermons were shorter on hellfire and damnation. The movement, not at first a church, was a breakaway from the United Secession Church and rejected its Calvinistic rigidities. Though initially espousing what it described as moderate Calvinism it gradually leaned more and more towards the rejection of Calvinism of any kind.

Christie was at an impressionable age when he encountered this movement, whose heartland was the countryside near his home. But it is unlikely that he would have gone as far as to train for its ministry but for the influence of one man: James Morison, the charismatic young preacher who was the founder of the Evangenlical Union. This man was to have a profound and enduring influence on Christie's life. 'There is no man living whom I respect so highly,' he was to write nearly 30 years later.[3]

Morison was still in his twenties when he first crossed Christie's path, but already his influence had been felt over much of Scotland. Ordained in the United Secession Church – an amalgam of various churches which had seceded from the Church of Scotland – he had rapidly developed a preaching style that was much more evangelical than that of his fellow ministers, and was not much to the liking of most of them. As a probationary minister in the North of Scotland he had attracted crowds and caused 'religious commotion' with his extemporary sermons in barns and mission halls. 'I never preach without seeing many wistful looks and moistened eyes,' he remarked.[4] He moved south in 1840 at a time when a revivalist movement was under way in Kilsyth and various other towns in the central belt of Scotland, so that the mood was receptive to his style of ministry when he was called to Clerk's Lane Church in Kilmarnock. The plain, substantial building could hold 1000 worshippers but on Sundays it couldn't contain the crowds drawn by Morison with 'his tall, erect form, with his large and finely developed head, his intellectual and cultured appearance, with a clear and melodious voice'.[5] The whole neighbourhood throbbed with excitement and Morison was the subject of conversation everywhere.

Certain members of his own church, however, were unimpressed. The United Secession Church did not look with favour on revivalist preaching or on Morison's unorthodox doctrines, particularly that of universal atonement: Christ died for the whole human race, he maintained, and not for some men only. In 1841 Kilmarnock Secession presbytery put him on him on trial for heresy – specifically for his rejection of the doctrine of predestination – and suspended him from the ministry and from membership of the church amid noisy scenes of disagreement in which windows were smashed and several pews gave way.[6] With public interest spreading rapidly out from Kilmarnock the church Synod endorsed the presbytery's action and appointed another preacher to fill the pulpit, but the Clerk's Lane congregation, which remained loyal to Morison, discovered that they owned the church, so he was able to keep his pulpit, his full salary and his manse.

His fame continued to grow. Invitations to preach came from towns and villages around Kilmarnock, including Strathaven, some miles away, with Morison sometimes preaching in the open air to crowds of 1500. He went on an evangelical tour as far afield as Carlisle. With other expelled ministers he formed the Evangelical Union in 1843 (the event was overshadowed by the Disruption [7] just two days later), and, moving further from the Calvinism of the Westminster Confession, they found sympathetic interest in the ranks of the Scottish Congregationalists, with whom they were to eventually unite.

With the Clerk's Lane Church overflowing with worshippers, new churches were formed, including one in Strathaven which was set up in 1844 with a minister, Alexander Cochrane Wood, who had been expelled from the Congregational academy in Glasgow for views similar to Morison's. This church formally joined the EU in 1846 [8] when Christie was in his late teens. Whether or not this was his first contact with the EU he was soon, under Morison's influence, to become totally committed to it and determined to become one of its ministers.

When he began his studies in August, 1850, the theological academy met in the session house of the Clerk's Lane Church. Started by Morison in 1843, it was highly valued as a feeder for the EU ministry, which was building new churches more rapidly than it could acquire ministers. This seems to have made Morison reluctant to expel any students who were not up to scratch (a category which did not include Christie). As one EU historian diplomatically put it, Morison was never pleased with less than the best but he had to make the most of the young men who came to be preachers and 'keep in mind the "supplies".' [9]

He ran a strict regime all the same, cramming a lot into the eight-week session, including classes in Hebrew and New Testament Greek, and setting a hefty programme of theological reading. Students were left with little leisure time. Classes began early in the morning and students had to be there on time. Latecomers were locked out and had to rap on the door for admission and then apologise. Morison, who did all the lecturing in the early years, even decreed which of the town's clocks was to be the official timekeeper. [10] He made a deep impression not only on Christie but on all the students. 'There were things about about him that made us feel we were in the presence of no ordinary man,' said one of them. [11] Christie, for one, was evidently influenced by one of the academy's rules – 'Cultivate courtesy and gentle habits' although this obviously never prevented the 'spurts of utterances' that erupted in his moments of anger.

There were only five students in Christie's class, one of whom later became a Baptist minister.[12] The academy's students were a close-knit, clannish group, thanks to their isolation from more orthodox Presbyterians. Because of the shortage of ministers in the rapidly expanding church many of them were pressed into service in the pulpit, so that contrary to the assumption of one of his obituarists, Christie probably did preach.

Not long after Christie began his studies Morrison moved to a church in Glasgow, and the academy moved with him. Probably it met at first in the new church's temporary accommodation in the Athaeneum in Ingram Street but by 1853 a new chapel had been built in North Dundas Street and the classes were held there.This was convenient for Christie, who had moved to Glasgow to begin his studies at Glasgow University. His mother had left Strathaven by this time and taken over a large flat in South St Mungo Street in the Calton area. Christie and his young brother Andrew, still serving his apprenticeship, moved in with her. The flat was shared by two lodgers of around Christie's own age – a baker's journeyman and a Glasgow University philosophy student. A tinsmith, a tanner, a victualler, and a horse-dealer were among their nearest neighbours.[13] The flat could not have been handier for the university, still on its medieval High Street site and on the doorstep of what were sometimes described as the worst slums in Europe. This overcrowded area, darkened by smoke and polluted with chemicals from nearby factories, had been among the worst affected parts of the city by the cholera epidemic that had struck just a couple of years before the Christies settled in Calton. Another cholera epidemic, the third to attack the city, struck before Christie had finished his arts course. This disease, with its high mortality, would one day play a dominant role in his life, but meanwhile his efforts were bent in other directions.

CHAPTER 3

Democratic intellect

Beginning his university studies in October 1850, immediately after the first session of his theological course, Christie was plunged into a very different world from the tightly knit community of Theological Academy scholars with their shared religious beliefs. Many of his fellow arts students were motivated by learning for its own sake – it was quite common at that time to attend only certain classes rather than undertake a course ending in graduation (the student in Mrs Christie's lodgings was an example of this trend). If the students had a common passion it was metaphysics. In between classes there were many 'long arguments over freedom of the will and other metaphysical topics to which the Scottish mind was prone', according to one of Christie's student contemporaries (who also, however, admitted that some students preferred to sharpen their wits in the nearby pubs).[1] With a philosophy student in the South St Mungo Street household, Christie would have had scope for metaphysical arguments at home as well as at college.

His classmates included students from a variety of social backgrounds. The middle-class element was stronger than national mythology would suggest.[2] Grants were non-existent and bursaries skimpy. Nevertheless some students from poorer families worked their way through college – one of the top students in the logic class spent much of the year as a blacksmith. Christie was by no means the only student to have reached his twenties before he had gathered together enough money to fund his studies.

Some of his fellow-students were destined for fame. James Bryce, with an illustrious career ahead of him as a scholar, member of Gladstone's cabinet, and Ambassador to the United States, was in the same ethics, philosophy and mathematics classes as Christie. Among students who would remain friends or associates for the rest of Christie's life was John Ross, future scholar and critic, teacher of English at the High School of Edinburgh, and editor of the popular *Globe Encyclopaedia*, to which Christie would one day contribute many hundreds of articles (thus bearing out a contemporary's wry observation that Ross 'had quite a peculiar power of turning to account the companionships of college life, which often count for more in a student's education than the direct instruction furnished in classrooms').[3] Another lasting friendship was with John Service, future minister of Hyndland Parish Church, which Christie attended in later life in preference to the Evangelical Union. Like many other future ministers Service was less than sedate in his student days – 'the humorous mentor of our extravagancies', according to one of his contemporaries who also described him as the student who had 'most native genius'.[4]

Christie did moderately well at his studies, coming fourth in Greek in his first year, and later landing the prize for an examination on studies done during the vacation. (Exams were always oral in these days and prizes usually awarded by class vote.) His teachers included Edward Lushington, the handsome if somewhat unkempt Professor of Greek, who was married to Tennyson's sister; William Ramsay, Professor of Latin, who was reckoned to be one of the finest teachers of his generation; Professor Robert Buchanan, a polished lecturer known as Logic Bob; and Hugh Blackburn, Professor of Mathematics, a fluent lecturer who never attempted to exercise authority – he merely sat down until the students stopped throwing paper darts.

Towards the end of his course Christie squeezed in a class on ecclesiastical history in the faculty of divinity under the remarkable Professor Thomas Thomson Jackson, known to his students as 'the holy ghost' because of his tall stooped figure and lank white hair. Sporting a tall silk hat he used to move rapidly about, looking straight ahead of him and disregarding everyone else. Every afternoon he could be seen walking with Mrs Jackson and her little dog. Although apt to be 'abstrusely metaphysical' in his lectures he placed great emphasis on essay-writing, which would certainly have suited Christie.[5]

He graduated BA (still at that time awarded in Scottish universities) in 1856 and in the same year was ordained as a minister in the Evangelical Union. Nearing 30, he seemed at last to be standing on the threshold of his career. But, as so often throughout his life, he did an about-turn just when things seemed settled. After returning to university for another year to gain his MA degree, and studying physics under William Thomson, the future Lord Kelvin, who was only five years his senior, he turned his back on the ministry. Apparently he had developed a 'weakness in the throat' which would have made him unsuited to the pulpit. Strangely, his religious mentor, James Morison, was struck by a similar affliction, which he blamed on the dampness of the North Dundas Street church.[6] Morison thereafter devoted himself more to writing than preaching, a change of emphasis that coincided with the ebbing of the original fervour of the EU (and indeed with revivalism throughout the country). Later in the century it would be absorbed into the Congregational Union. Perhaps Christie's own fervour had begun to ebb too, though he maintained a certain connection with the EU to the end of his life. At any rate, he decided on a complete change of plan. He would become a doctor.

CHAPTER 4
Dr Christie

C HRISTIE was 28 when he started his medical studies. Mrs Christie, still taking in lodgers, may have been less than delighted to hear that her son was committing himself to four more years of study. Moreover the prospect of having a doctor in the family was possibly no great compensation – medical men did not enjoy a very high social status in the commercial atmosphere of mid-nineteenth-century Glasgow.

Christie was 'looked up to as "old"' by his fellow-students, one of whom later remembered him as a 'somewhat prim and precise personality'.[1] His restrained manner was at odds with the prevailing image of the Glasgow medical students. According to one of his Arts Faculty contemporaries, of all the students at that time 'the medicals were the roughest and led the least orderly lives.'[2]

The Medical Faculty itself was not basking in glory in those days. Its reputation had declined from the heights that it had attained during the Enlightenment. Lister, who would help to bring it once again to international prominence, did not arrive on the scene till the year after Christie graduated. Reforms designed to bring about uniform standards throughout the country were introduced during his student days, mainly through the Medical Act of 1858, but did not affect his own degree course – he was among the last students to graduate with the old MD degree, soon to be supplanted by the MB, CM (Master of Surgery).

All the same Christie had some fine teachers, a few of them imbued with the same philosophical spirit and generalist approach as their

40

Enlightenment predecessors. Among them was the internationally renowned eye surgeon William Mackenzie, founder of Glasgow Eye Infirmary and once described by a fellow-doctor as 'the last great man of the old school' as well as 'a man of keen penetration and of the scientific spirit'.[3] Christie did well in his class, winning first prize for his essay on 'The Physiology of the Iris'. He picked up more prizes in medicine than he had in his arts course, generally for essays rather than exams. The only class prize that he won was in Professor Andrew Buchanan's class on the theory of medicine. Buchanan regarded exams as futile and placed his reliance on essays – sometimes with unexpected results, it was claimed. Christie also won several prizes for his lecture notes. His habits of mind were obviously as precise as his manner.

Like other medical students Christie also spent time at Glasgow Royal Infirmary, visiting the wards and assisting the physicians. It was there that he made the acquaintance of a man who would one day become one of his closest friends and colleagues: James Burn Russell, Glasgow's future Medical Officer of Health. Russell, a year behind Christie in his studies, later remarked that 'Christie's personal appearance and manner declared the man as experience found him to be. Of middle height, exact in dress, quiet in gait, he always had himself well in hand, speaking with great precision and calmness in a somewhat low voice, in short, emphatic sentences'. But when he came to know him better Russell also observed Christie's 'great spurts of utterances' when roused – as happened quite often, as his controversial career was to show.[4]

Christie graduated in 1860 at the age of 30. With his precision and attention to detail, plus his fine performance in William Mackenzie's class, he might have seemed well suited to specialise in ophthalmology. But Christie was never predictable. Soon he was heading off in a very different direction. Leaving the South St Mungo Street household he became briefly a resident assistant at the Royal Infirmary and also assistant physician at the University Lying-in Hospital in George Street, in which role he contributed to the *Glasgow Medical Journal* his first effort in a lifetime of published work – an account of an obstetric case in which a noose of worsted yarn had been tied round the baby's foot to provide traction in the absence of contractions. But within two years he had left both these posts to become assistant physician at what was then called Glasgow Lunatic Asylum (the future Gartnavel Royal Hospital). It was assumed by colleagues that he had taken this step on the advice of one of the physicians at the Lying-in Hospital, John Pagan, Professor of Midwifery at Glasgow University and a practitioner with 'an exceptional gift of intuitive diagnosis'.[5] Pagan had once given an extra-mural course on 'the medical jurisprudence of insanity' and his name often appeared on the admission documents of Gartnavel patients. Christie possibly also visited the asylum as an undergraduate. By the late 1850s a limited number of medical students were visiting the wards.[6]

The post was residential. For the next three years Christie's home was the resplendently turreted Tudor Gothic building in its country setting well to the west of the city boundary. Designed by the architect Charles Wilson to replace the old Glasgow Asylum in Dobbie's Loan, it had been opened for less than two decades when Christie took up his post. Private patients were housed in the West wing, paupers in the East, the former enjoying turkey dinners at Christmas while the latter ate meagre meat pies. Basic hygiene was rudimentary, with sewage still running into cesspits. Just before Christie arrived the asylum had been connected to the new Loch Katrine water supply, but water was an expensive commodity and in the 1860s the same bathwater was generally shared by four patients.[7]

The physician-superintendent in Christie's day was Alexander Mackintosh, who had fought off strong competition for this coveted post, for the asylum's standing was high. Mackintosh is remembered as probably the first superintendent to have undertaken the clinical teaching of psychiatry at Gartnavel and also for his rejection of the policy of physical restraint by straitjackets and other devices.[8]

Christie's life at Gartnavel was hard. There was only one other resident assistant, David Gilland, a future superintendant of Berkshire County Asylum who had been in Christie's year at Glasgow University. The two junior doctors began their rounds of the male wards before

7 a.m. 'to see the state of the patients and their apartments, and to do what may be necessary for their welfare.'[9] They wrote detailed case notes for the visiting physician and surgeon. Christie, who had won university prizes for his lecture notes, wrote meticulous notes which are easy to distinguish from Gilland's more scrawling hand. They sometimes make poignant reading. Many of the patients seem to have been suffering from delusions. A bank clerk was convinced he was the king of Scotland; a weaver believed he was Mungo Park; and a woman thought that people were coming through the walls. Sometimes there were attempted escapes. A ship's engineer thought he had made a clean break until he fell in with two women, not realising that they were asylum attendants sent out to lure him back.[10]

Life at Gartnavel was not all grim. There was a tremendous outbreak of jollification when the Prince of Wales married Princess Alexandra in 1863. The towers and parapets of the asylum were brilliantly illuminated in the form of St Andrew's and St George's crosses, Chinese lanterns were suspended over the main entrance and an illumination of the Prince of Wales's coronet plus the initials of bride and groom glittered over the entrance to East House, the paupers' part of the asylum. The bell 'rang a merry peal' while an army of patients, headed by the asylum band and two kilted pipers, marched round the grounds. The patients were 'sumptuously regaled', according to the annual report.[11] Christie is unlikely to have joined in the celebrations with much enthusiasm, particularly since later events showed that he was not an admirer of Queen Victoria and her family.

Both Christie and Gilland were praised by the directors for their zeal and ability and at the end of their first year at Gartnavel were given salary increases.[12] Christie possibly saw his Gartnavel work mainly as useful experience for a future medical practice, but he was genuinely interested in psychological medicine. With help from Gilland, who soon became a friend, he set about writing a paper entitled 'On Suicidal Impulse'. A large proportion of Gartnavel patients were considered to have suicidal tendencies – 71 out of the 225 residents, according to the report for 1863.[13] Christie classified them according to motive and intention, distinguishing, for example, between people who acted out of remorse and those who were attempting to escape from an imaginary horror. One patient had begged to have his stomach cut open to let out the rats, and Christie was certain that if there had been a knife to hand the man would have attempted to do this himself. The paper was published in the *Glasgow Medical Journal* in October, 1864.[14] It would have made a good start to a career in psychological medicine. But it was actually Christie's farewell to this field, though he remained interested in suicide for the rest of his career. By the time the paper was published he had already left Gartnavel after only four years at his post.

General practice would have been the obvious next step, but Christie was never predictable. Before deciding on his next career move he spent a year in Paris, studying at the city's hospitals and also making visits to hospitals in Leipzig and Vienna. In Paris he was particularly impressed when a scarred old French army veteran showed him round two outlying convalescent homes, one for men and one for women, to which patients were brought from city hospitals to have 'both body and mind invigorated by a month's residence in a pleasant and healthy locality, where every possible attention is paid to them'. He wrote to the *Glasgow Herald* giving his impressions and advocating similar residences for Glasgow.[15]

When he returned to Scotland his mother was on her deathbed. Mrs Christie had earlier left the South St Mungo Street flat to keep house for her son Andrew, who had managed to save up enough money to buy an ironmonger's business in Kilmarnock. His fellow shopkeepers in Duke Street were impressed when they watched him emerge in shirt sleeves to wash the windows whenever the painters began changing the shop sign. Andrew, who was still a bachelor at the age of 31, lived in a house in Princes Street, Kilmarnock, and it was there that Mary Christie died from an abdominal tumour at the age of 73 in June, 1865. Her son James was with her and signed the death certificate.

After his mother's death he was still in restless mood. Instead of settling down to general practice or hospital work he made another of his unpredictable moves. He decided to go to Zanzibar.

CHAPTER 5
Anglicans and Africans

Little more than two months after his mother's death Christie set sail from Greenock to join the Universities Mission to Central Africa, an Anglican mission formed by the universities of Oxford, Cambridge, Dublin and Durham. The previous year it had retreated from a disastrous foray into the Zambezi to make Zanzibar its base for further operations. Christie signed on as honorary physician. The mission's first doctor, John Dickinson, had died of fever after about two years at his post.

Christie's move was probably not the result of a sudden impulse. David Livingstone, who would one day play a significant role in his life, had been in Glasgow when Christie was a medical student. He arrived in the city as a national hero after his historic trudge across Africa from the Atlantic to the Indian Ocean. This was the first European passage through the heart of Africa and it caught the imagination of a public which had until then supposed that Southern Africa was a desert like the Sahara. The incipient myth that Livingstone had converted thousands of 'savages' to Christianity contributed to his celebrity status. In London, he had to be careful where he went so as not to be mobbed. Once he narrowly escaped being crushed by a crowd in Regent Street. When he was recognised in church, people would clamber over the pews to shake his hand and the service would be abandoned in chaos. He was given a hero's welcome on his lecture tour of the country.[1] In speeches in Oxford and Cambridge he appealed to young men to dedicate themselves to a life of service in Africa. This was to lead to the establishment of the Universities Mission.[2]

Livingstone's call to youth was repeated a little later when he addressed an eager audience of Glasgow University students in February, 1858. With his weathered appearance and his slow, deliberate way of speaking he commanded total attention. He talked of his work and his plans and said that he looked to the students as the men of the next generation to carry these out.[3]

Christie, in the middle of his medical studies and with financial obligations to his mother, was in no position to respond. And when Livingstone returned to Glasgow early in 1864, having spent the intervening years exploring the Zambezi, Christie was hard at work in Gartnavel, absorbed in investigating the suicidal impulse. But when his mother died in the early summer of 1865, Livingstone was still in Britain, organising support for his next African exploration. After the failure of his Zambezi expedition he had been given a generally more subdued reception than on his previous visit but he was still warmly welcomed in Scotland.[4]

It would have been surprising if Christie had not felt a measure of fellow-feeling for the explorer. The two had strikingly similar backgrounds, though Christie was the younger by 16 years. Both came from Lanarkshire families of limited means, both had had to work before becoming students, and both had studied medicine in Glasgow (Livingstone at the Andersonian University) while also taking classes in theology. Both were nonconformists: Livingstone's father was a member of the Hamilton branch of Christie's church, the Evangelical Union. Livingstone himself was a member of the Congregational Union, which had a close affinity with the Evangelical Union and was eventually to merge with it. Above all, Christie had the restless urge and curiosity of an explorer, as future events would prove.

There was also a personal link. His mother's lodgers in South St Mungo Street had latterly included Robert Livingston, a young man in the same trade as Christie's brother Andrew. In Christie's nephew's memoirs he is described as a cousin of David Livingstone's. He was certainly not a first cousin, and appears in none of the published family trees. His mother's surname, Lawrie, suggests that he might have been more distantly related on that side of the family for one of David Livingstone's aunts on his father's side had married into the Lawrie family of Blantyre. Robert Livingston was to become a close lifelong friend of both the Christie brothers.

Whatever his motives, Christie was making a courageous move. He was 36 and finally launched on a promising medical career. His first paper had just been published in a professional journal. He had won plaudits for his work at Gartnavel and was well positioned for promotion. Moreover he had no knowledge of tropical medicine. When he was about to leave for Zanzibar he heard reports that a cholera epidemic was heading for the island and consulted a friend, Dr John McLatchie, who had worked in a temporary fever hospital in Glasgow during the 1848-9 epidemic. As it happened the 1865 epidemic in East Africa was blocked by an unseasonably early monsoon before it reached Zanzibar (though the same pandemic did reach Glasgow, shortly after Christie had left). But McLatchie's notes were to be needed in due course.

To make matters worse the mission that Christie was joining had got off to an unhappy start. Launched with considerable fanfare by Gladstone and Wilberforce in 1859, it prepared for action. In 1861 a party under the leadership of Bishop Charles Mackenzie set sail in high spirits to establish a mission station in a spot chosen by Livingstone in what later became Malawi. The mood began to change when Livingstone met them at the mouth of the Zambezi. His Zambezi expedition, launched three years before the mission party arrived, had not been going well. Indecisive leadership and violent quarrels between Livingstone and his brother Charles had destroyed morale.[5] Livingstone's hopes that the Zambezi would become 'God's highway to the interior' had proved unrealistic and he had turned his attention instead to the Shire River.

Livingstone had more in mind than exploration. He had become the prophet of late-Victorian imperialism. Increasingly convinced that

Christianity and commerce went hand in hand, he believed that an organised colony was the only way forward. Legitimate trade would undermine the slave trade and set the scene for the spread of Christianity.The Industrial Revolution was, he believed, part of a divine plan. It seemed to him that the uplands above the Shire river were eminently suitable for cotton growing, sugar manufacture and other industries and in dispatches to the Foreign Office he urged in vain that a British colony be established.[6] But his assessment was too optimistic. The Shire highlands were devastated by drought and by the effects of tribal wars resulting from the slave trade[7] but Livingstone was unwilling to admit that the area was unsuitable for a mission station: this would have given the game away.

He also welcomed the prospect of a mission headed by a bishop, which would almost amount to a kind of territorial claim on the area. Bishop Mackenzie, once described as 'an energetic and hearty man in the best traditions of muscular Christianity',[8] prodded slacking porters with his crozier during the 70-mile march to the mission station at Magomero but soon had worse problems to face. Three of the six missionaries accompanying him died of malaria after their supplies of quinine were lost when a canoe capsized. Mackenzie himself died in 1862, shortly before Livingstone's wife Mary, who had come out to join her husband, succumbed to malaria. Mackenzie's successor, Bishop William George Tozer, arrived on the scene and was dismayed to find that the work of the mission had become 'merely a struggle to survive', with scant missionary work accomplished. 'The Zambezi has proved in every way a miserable failure, and the selection of it for English missionary work can only be due to the blindest enthusiasm,' he wrote to the Bishop of Cape Town. Tozer was also deeply opposed to Livingstone's aim of colonisation and was glad that the attempt had failed. 'In planting an English village here . . . you must run the risk of introducing English bad habits as well as English virtues,' he pointed out. In his view missionary work, pure and simple, should be the objective.[9]

He attempted to relocate the mission station at a site in the highlands of the Upper Shire but finding it 'no place for a Church of

England mission' decided to cut the mission's losses and retreat from the Shire altogether. After considering various options he decided that Zanzibar would be the best base. This move brought down on his head 'the fierce wrath' of David Livingstone, who accused the bishop of cowardice. Tozer, he said, was acting just as St Augustine would have done had he located himself in the Channel Islands when sent to convert the natives of England. Tozer felt that if he had kept the mission on the mainland for fear of being called a coward, the accusation would have been justified.[10] Livingstone, whose Government-sponsored expedition was recalled soon afterwards, continued to view Tozer as a deserter and refused to regard the bishop's continuing work in Zanzibar as part of the original enterprise (for good measure he privately mocked Tozer's ecclesiastical garb[11] and said that he 'seems no more fit to be a missionary than I am to be captain of a man of war'[12]). The move to Zanzibar broke Livingstone's cherished link between commerce and Christianity, of which Tozer so strongly disapproved.

In selecting Zanzibar as the future headquarters Tozer was rejecting advice from the mission's committees in Oxford and Cambridge, who favoured Zululand. Zanzibar, in Tozer's view, was ideal because it had good communications with the Cape and India and was the entrepot of the East coast of Africa: the trade routes radiating out from the island would make it a superb springboard for missions to the mainland. It also had a British consul and a friendly Sultan. And, declared Tozer, there was 'generally something going on to amuse the mind'.[13]

He arrived in Zanzibar town in the late summer of 1864, accompanied by a single colleague, Dr Edward Steere – the sickly survivors of the original mission, who had been recruited by Bishop Mackenzie, declined to accompany them. Soon afterwards a large house overlooking the sea was rented from the Sultan of Zanzibar for use as a mission school and the Sultan – 'our staunch friend' – provided its first pupils, former slaves. The consulate surgeon, Edward Seward, offered to provide free medical services to the missionaries and their pupils – but this was only an interim arrangement.[14] A few months later it was agreed that James Christie would join the mission as honorary physician.

Christie, in taking this step into the unknown, was joining a highly unusual as well as controversial venture. This was the first African mission to be run by a bishop in Africa rather than by committees at home, and the first mission dedicated to training Africans as clergymen rather than simply converting them. As an ordained minister in the Evangelical Union, Christie would obviously be odd man out in a mission that was not merely Anglican but decidedly High Church. But mission work tended to minimise doctrinal and denominational differences, as Livingstone himself noted. 'The feelings which we have towards different sects alter out here quite insensibly, till one looks upon all godly men as good and true brethern,' he once wrote to a friend.[15]

Livingstone, with a religious profile very similar to Christie's, had been willing to work with Anglicans and indeed thought that episcopal organisation was particularly suited to mission work (the Church of Scotland, still preoccupied with internal affairs after the Disruption of 1843, was not a major player in the field at that time). Christie's enthusiasm for religious revivalism had probably waned by this time, and in any case, as honorary physician, he was to be engaged only in medical work. Moreover, his services to the mission, which were to be unpaid, would be only a small part of his work. He would earn his living from private practice in Zanzibar Town and from additional work as doctor to the only British company on the island, which had a sugar plantation and factory with a large workforce in the north of the island.

This arrangement had apparently been made when Christie had met the proprietor, the remarkable Captain Hugh Fraser, in Glasgow. Fraser, a former officer in the Indian Navy, had developed business interests in Zanzibar after the disbandment of the Indian Navy in 1863. A charming but untrustworthy man, and a born troublemaker, he would play an important part in Christie's life in Zanzibar and his plausible account of the bright prospects there might even have influenced the doctor's decision to embark on this adventure. Christie can hardly have known that Fraser's business was becoming deeply embroiled in controversy just at the time he signed on as its doctor.

He was in optimistic mood when he embarked for his three-month journey round the Cape of Good Hope. 'Everything indicates a most comfortable and agreeable passage,' he wrote to his brother Andrew as the sailing ship passed Portpatrick in fine weather. The letter, to be taken ashore by the tug which was taking the ship as far as the Isle of Man, was the first of about 150 that Christie would write to his brother in Kilmarnock before his return to Scotland nine years later.[16]

CHAPTER 6
Zanzibar

CHRISTIE was relieved when Zanzibar was at last sighted, in late November, 1865. He had wearied of life on board ship – it was 'very tiresome to be sailing every day and to see nothing but sea and sky'. He was delighted with his first view of the coastline with its 'pretty bays with a border of sand of the most dazzling whiteness' and with tall coconut trees giving the island a tropical appearance. He was agreeably impressed by the view of Zanzibar town from the sea, standing on a triangular spit of land with its white, flat-roofed Arab houses lining the waterfront. The Sultan's palace rose above the other buildings and the flags of Britain, the US, France and the Hanseatic countries flew from the consulate roofs.

The town, he later reported to his brother, was 'truly oriental' in appearance: Zanzibar was an Arab state, and all the Europeans lived in Moorish-style houses fronting the sea. Christie found the architecture difficult to get used to when settling into the seafront house belonging to Captain Fraser's company – Fleming, Fraser and Co. – which was to be his home for the time being. It had a row of arches supporting a lofty ceiling and rather than rooms in the ordinary sense had a series of corridors round an open courtyard.[1] Other occupants of these fine waterfront buildings included rich Arabs, western diplomats, and, of course, the Universities Mission. Behind the waterfront houses was a labyrinth of bazaars where Indian merchants lived and a maze of crooked narrow alleys crowded with Africans pulling handcarts and hawkers shouting for custom. The streets, Christie observed, were so narrow that there was scarcely room for two donkeys with their panniers to pass each other.[2] Here and there an elaborately carved wooden doorway would signify the home of a well-to-do merchant. Christie perhaps took a less romantic view of the scene than Dr Edward Steere, of the Universities Mission, who was constantly reminded of the *Arabian Nights* by the white-robed Arabs with their turbans and coats of blue and scarlet, the rich people with elaborately carved daggers stuck in the shawls round their waists and the 'peeps of arches and courtyards mixed in among a rough and ruinous effect'.[3] Bishop Tozer, striding along in his crimson clerical garb, added an extra touch of colour.

Christie had little opportunity to explore at first. Mosquito bites on his legs and feet became so inflamed that for about two weeks he was unable to put his feet on the ground. But by early January he was fit for work and although it was the hot season he felt comfortable in his thin woollen shirt and loose trousers. 'I like this place very well – indeed much better than I expected,' he wrote to Andrew.[4]

Zanzibar at that time was no backwater. It had grown in the previous three decades from an insignificant off-shore island to be the principal port on the western shores of the Indian Ocean. In the harbour square-rigged vessels from the West lay alongside Arab dhows with sails of every colour. On shore, a New England merchant might be seen exchanging American cloth for ivory with a turban-wearing Indian while a trader from Marseilles haggled with a Somali.[5] Growing international demand for gum copal, a resin used for varnish in the manufacture of furniture, had allowed local traders to set advantageous terms.[6] Zanzibar had also become the supplier of most of the world's cloves but its increase in wealth and influence was due less to the produce of its plantations than to its traffic in ivory and slaves transported along newly extended trade routes to the interior. Each year the slave masters brought in tens of thousands of emaciated Africans from the interior to be chained to the block in the huge open-air slave market in Zanzibar town and, after being subjected to brutal indignities by potential purchasers, auctioned to Arab dealers in flowing robes.[7] Most were then exported to Arab countries.

This trade was deeply rooted in the island's culture. Arab colonies had been planted along the East African coast as early as the eighth century and Africans were captured and sold to countries where Islamic law prohibited the hiring of Muslims as slaves. The Portuguese gained control in the sixteenth century but after the downfall of their empire the Arabs of Oman asserted their overlordship of the Zanzibar archipelago and large tracts of the mainland. Seyyid Said, who became one of the outstanding rulers of the Arab world, shifted his seat of government from Oman to Zanzibar in 1840 in order to pursue his African ambitions. His dynamic policy transformed the island. He encouraged clove planting, concluded commercial treaties with the US, Britain and France and provided for the establishment of western consulates. He fostered the growth of the Indian community and made use of its services in his administration. Not least, he encouraged the slave and ivory trades through a rapid extension of the old Arab caravan routes into the interior.[8] As the price paid for British naval help in discouraging French incursions in the area Seyyid Said had to agree to restrictions in the export of slaves but in the mid-1860s, when Christie came to Zanzibar, Said's successor, the less dynamic Sultan Majid, still derived a large part of his revenue from the import and export duties on this trade.

At that time the population of the island was around 300,000, an estimate based on the rough calculations of western diplomats since the Arab ruling class kept no records. The Arabs, numbering only about 4000, consisted of a landed aristocracy of plantation owners descended from the Omani settlers, plus Arabs from the Hadramaut who arrived regularly to find work as porters. The Indian population, also thought to be about 4000, though estimates varied, came mainly from British India or from the Indian states under British protection and remained under the jurisdiction of the Bombay Government. Most were Muslims, principally of the Khoja community, but there were also a few hundred Hindus or Banyan Indians, including many influential financiers and traders, the merchant princes of Zanzibar. The bulk of the island's population was made up of some 220,000

Africans, most of whom were slaves working either in the plantations or in private houses. A few thousand of these were descended from Zanzibar's original inhabitants, the Hadimi and the Tumbatu, but most had been captured and brought to Zanzibar from so many different tribes in the interior that they had to learn Swahili (a Bantu language with many Arab loan words) in order to understand one another.

In addition there were some five dozen western residents – diplomats, traders, missionaries – about 20 of whom were British. The Americans, exporting cotton cloth from Massachusetts, had established an early dominance in trade,[9] and it was partly to challenge this that a British consulate had been established in 1841, the first western diplomatic mission in Zanzibar. The British presence was also intended to serve strategic interests by safeguarding the sea routes to India and curbing French ambitions in the area. It also enabled Zanzibar's Indian community, who were still considered British subjects, to be brought under the control of the Bombay Government, which appointed the consul and used him as its political agent (although the consulate also increasingly corresponded with the Foreign Office in London).[10] Not least, it was reckoned that the consulate would be able to bring pressure on the Sultan to end the slave trade, and a step in that direction was taken in a treaty of 1843 which outlawed the export of slaves beyond his African territories.

Christie's patients were drawn from all these ethnic groups, although not in equal measures. His only African patients appear to have been surgical cases, and the bulk of his practice consisted of Banyan Indians, a community for whom he had a huge liking and respect. He realised that with their impressive business acumen they were the ones who really ruled Zanzibar.

Although Christie had the services of an interpreter he set about learning Swahili to help him communicate with his patients. He had also to familiarise himself with their customs and religious practices. He was taught a sharp lesson by his very first patient, a Banyan (Hindu) Indian whose ears needed a good clean-out. When Christie advanced with a syringe of water the man gave a loud cry and fled. The Banyans, he quickly learned, had strict rules about water – it had to be drawn from their own wells and by a member of their own caste or they would consider themselves defiled. When Banyans had to be given medicine in solution they would, Christie recorded, bring their own bottles of water wrapped in a white cloth so that the contents couldn't be seen. And when water had to be given to a Banyan Indian who was feeling faint it was drunk behind a large scarf held up as a screen. It was said that the patient would tip back his head and pour the water into his mouth without touching the vessel.[11]

Arab patients posed different problems. Christie was astonished to find their sickrooms crowded with relatives and friends who considered that their attendance was 'as necessary as if it were in response to a call to arms'.[12] African patients, however, posed the reverse problem – Christie was sometimes unable to persuade relatives to care for the sick and dying. When bribes failed he was reduced to threats of beatings. In a letter to his brother he attempted to defend his actions by saying: 'Here we merely threaten, but in Glasgow the magistrates carry it into effect on the backs of the small boys who steal loaves to satisfy their cravings.'[13]

His patients also included most of the five or six dozen European residents in Zanzibar town and sailors on visiting ships in the harbour, whom Christie regarded as his best paying patients. The British consulate, which had been established in 1841 in an effort to prevent the US's rapidly developing trade turning into political domination, had its own doctor (but Christie was once called in as an expert witness in a rape trial in the consular court). The Universities Mission, however, kept him particularly busy – its members, who quickly increased from the initial two to around six or seven, seemed particularly prone to illness.

Christie's medical supplies came from two Glasgow apothecaries (in the Trongate and Rutherglen Road) and were made up from lists sent by Christie to his brother, along with requests for – typically – two dozen white shirts, one dozen white neckties, six pairs of boots, a black tile hat, a dozen pairs of white drill trousers, and two white linen umbrellas, 'all of the best quality', and some *Glasgow Herald*s.[14] He also asked Andrew to inquire about the cost of an apparatus for the manufacture of castor oil since the seeds could be obtained cheaply in Zanzibar.

The medicines would be badly needed before long. Christie didn't regard Zanzibar as totally unhealthy but it was certainly unsanitary, with a dangerous potential for spreading disease. When he looked out acoss the Indian Ocean from the top of the house the view was idyllic, not least at the setting of the sun, but when he looked down to the beach he saw it being used as a public convenience by Africans of both sexes and even some merchant princes. The somewhat prim Christie was especially outraged that this took place 'under the very windows of houses where European ladies are resident'.[15] Some visitors vomited when they saw the beach, where rotting corpses lay.

As a student and as a houseman at the Royal Infirmary he must have seen appalling conditions in the closes and wynds near the High Street, whose slums were sometimes said to be the worst in Europe. But nothing had prepared him for what he saw in Zanzibar Town. 'The sanitary condition of Zanzibar is as bad as bad can be,' he declared later in the book that he wrote soon after he returned to Glasgow, which was to become the classic account of conditions in Zanzibar at that time and which is still much quoted in histories of the island and travel writing.[16] There were no sanitary regulations at all, he noted, because there was no taxation to provide the funds and no political will to impose even quarantine regulations. There were no sewers. Latrines were just shallow pits. When one became blocked by the accumulations of a generation or two it was either closed up and new ones excavated or, to quote Christie, 'the slimy, semi-solid contents are baled out on the public streets and left to find their way by the nearest slope towards the sea beach by the laws of gravitation.' One putrid, slimy mass, emptied from a public building, was 'allowed to pursue its snail-like course to the lagoon, along half the breadth of the town' forcing pedestrians either to walk through 'the abominable mass' or take to intricate side lanes.

The torrents which poured through the dirty streets during the monsoon months helped to clear the filth; and so did countless ants and beetles, millions of rats and armies of wild dogs. 'The wild dogs become ravenous and dangerous after sunset, and they have frequently attacked human beings trespassing on their haunts,' he reported, noting that the dogs became more dangerous when there were fewer corpses on the beach. 'At such times,' he added, 'it is dangerous to be on the streets at night, as they parade the town in search of garbage, but without their excellent services as public scavengers, the town would be scarcely habitable.'

Not all the filth was cleared – and none of it was removed for agricultural purposes. Ruined houses were converted into dung hills, as were the spaces between houses and bits of the beach.[17] The smells were very different from the scents nowadays associated with the spice island.

The drinking water matched the smells. Christie described it as 'the diluted drainage of dunghills, a saturated solution of every conceivable abomination'. He didn't change his opinion after the part-time US consul, Francis Webb, a New England merchant, agreed to send samples from the town wells to Salem, Massachusetts, for analysis. Even the best of the samples instantly blackened the lead paper held at the nose of the bottle. The only difference between the wells and the cesspools, Christie concluded, was that the wells were deeper.[18] Although bad sanitation might not give rise to an epidemic, he pointed out, if one did occur everything was conducive to its spread.

And so it was to prove all too quickly.

CHAPTER 7

Alarms and Excursions

D AVID LIVINGSTONE, who had left Britain in the same month as Christie, arrived in Zanzibar via Bombay in January, 1866, to prepare for the expedition that would turn out to be his last. 'This is the finest place I have known in all of Africa,' he wrote, '. . . an illusive place where nothing is as it seems. I am mesmerised.' But he loathed the smells. 'Stinkibar' was his nickname for the place. Occupying a small wooden house on the flat roof of the British consulate he was obviously in the front line for pestilential odours from the beach. At night he found the stench so gross 'that one might cut out a slice and manure a garden with it'. Christie, who had several meetings with him, noted that he was 'very sensitive to smells, and was thoroughly disgusted with the odours of the place'.[1]

He had a few reservations about the explorer. 'Dr Livingstone is a very energetic man,' he wrote in one of his letters to Kilmarnock, 'but I do not think that he expresses in public his private opinions. Christie was also inclined to downplay the significance of Livingstone's expeditions. 'There are many people in Zanzibar,' he wrote in the same letter, 'who are as familiar with the journey to the lake regions as you are with that to Strathaven, and they cannot understand what the English make such a fuss about.'[2]

Livingstone, not surprisingly, disapproved of Christie's threats of beatings to force Africans to care for sick relatives. 'You take the wrong way,' he said (as quoted by Christie). 'You should try and find one of the same tribe, and then you will see they attend to one another. Christie did so with one patient and found 'no difference whatever'. Not one of the patient's tribe, he reported, 'would go near her, or have anything to do with her'.[3]

Livingstone completed his preparations within two months and left for the interior. Several of Christie's obituaries state that he was the last white man to see the explorer before he left for his last journey, but that honour must belong to the officers of HMS *Penguin*, who transported him to the mainland and watched him march off inland.[4] Seven years later, though, Christie could claim a more melancholy distinction, as the doctor who first identified Livingstone's remains when they were brought back to Zanzibar,

Meanwhile, Christie's life had its lighter moments during those early months on the island. He found himself in a lively social set. The explorer Richard Burton, who visited Zanzibar less than a decade before Christie's arrival, noted that the European residents demonstrated 'a natural tendency towards drinking and drug taking, either of opium or hemp, and a descent into voluptuousness'. There is no indication that drugs were ever taken in Captain Fraser's establishment but he certainly kept a well-stocked cellar. There were generally three or four British men-of-war in the harbour, and their officers evidently preferred Fraser's table to meals on board. Christie painted the scene for his brother: 'Every day we have a party of officers at dinner, this house being looked upon as their headquarters on shore, and very nice jolly fellows they are, great hands at drinking pale ale, brandy and soda water.' He added that the house boasted a soda-water-making machine and that the senior officer on the station spent a day every now and then making and bottling 'the precious fluid'.[5]

Several months later when Christie rented a house of his own – also on the waterfront, not far from the Customs House – he was obviously determined to be an equally stylish host. A complete dinner set, ivory-handled knives and spoons, and an electro-plated cake basket were on the list of necessities posted to Andrew, and he added: 'In regard to crystal, you must send me toddy tumblers for beer, Hock glasses, coloured wine glasses, champagne glasses . . .' He also asked for lamps, ornaments for the table, and an iron bedstead with posts for a mosquito net – plus, if possible, 'the top of a shower bath' though he thought that if necessary he might be able to improvise one for himself.[6]

Not all his friends and acquaintances were European. One Hindu 'was a firm friend of mine from the day I landed in Zanzibar to the day I left' and he kept in touch with his Swahili teacher, Mohammed, after his return to Scotland, giving his views on the slavery question, the future of East Africa and other subjects that they had obviously discussed in Zanzibar 'when you were grinding me up in Swahili language and literature'. He also recalled how Mohammed had given him a book called *The Devil's Dictionary* and how he had found its 'pleasing and highly suggestive' phrases of courtship an agreeable change from the theological terms in Swahili that Dr Steere, of the Universities Mission, had given him to study.[7]

He also became acquainted with the Sultan, who invited him on hippopotamus-shooting parties, presented him with his photograph, called on him to attend his sick captain and dying brother, and made him physician to his army and navy, with uniform to match. Obviously the Sultan had not been too upset when Christie, granted an audience soon after his arrival in Zanzibar, arrived improperly clad – his tile hat had been crushed during the voyage, and he had been unable to buy or borrow another. Sultan Majid, Christie duly reported to Kilmarnock, lived in good style – 'his stable contains some two hundred horses and there is no difficulty getting one for a ride.'[8]

He took full advantage of this privilege, sending home for two pairs of white cord trousers and the best leather gaiters. At sunset and before daybreak he rode through the long jungle grass, soaked by the copious dews which were the great moisture fertilisers of the island. He liked to quench his thirst with coconut water, which after sunset was quickly cooled by rapid evaporation from the thick husk, forming 'a delightful and cooling drink'[9] (and a good antidote, perhaps, to Captain Fraser's brandy and soda).

Majid, of frail physic, indolent, and described once as 'nervous, moody and shifty,'[10] must have made a rather edgy companion at times. He had been having a troubled and anxious time of it since becoming Sultan in 1856. His father, the great Sayyid Said, had divided his realm in two, bequeathing his African dominions to Majid and his Arab lands to Majid's elder brother, Thwain. The settlement angered Thwain, who challenged the legality of the division, refused to be softened by Majid's offer of an annual tribute, and sailed for Zanzibar with an expeditionary force. It was intercepted and turned back by a British ship and Thwain caused no more trouble.[11]

But Majid's younger brother, Barghash, now declared open rebellion and started felling palm trees to make a stockade round a house called 'Marseilles' in the Zanzibar countryside. Anarchy spread through the island, houses were burned and looted, clove plantations were destroyed. Barghash had received encouragement from France, which hoped to undermine the diplomatic ascendancy that Britain had gained in Zanzibar, but Majid successfully appealed to the British Consul for help. The consul, Colonel Rigby, personally led a detachment of marines to Barghash's house, ordered rifle fire to be opened, then rapped on the door with his walking stick. Barghash surrendered and was sent into exile in Bombay.[12]

But even with the removal of these two threats Majid continued to feel insecure. Around the time when Christie first met him he had started to build a bolthole on the mainland, personally supervising the construction of a palace, a fort, and official residences at a spot 45 miles south of Zanzibar which he called Dar-es-Salaam – 'harbour of peace'.[13] Christie approved of the idea but doubted whether Majid would have the energy to go through with it.

Majid's ambitious and vastly expensive scheme fell through because of labour shortages: when the slaves were brought to the mainland they simply took themselves off and headed home to the interior. Meanwhile, family matters were again adding to Majid's problems. One of his favourite sisters, Princess Salme, who lived in a house opposite the German consulate, had an affair with a young part-time member of the consulate staff, Heinriche Ruete, a businessman from Hamburg. They are thought to have conversed from their balconies on either side of the narrow street and arranged countryside assignations. In the summer of 1866 it became apparent that Salme was pregnant and to escape retribution for her liaison with a Christian she planned to leave the island secretly. The princess, much liked in the British community, found a willing collaborator in Captain Malcolm Pasley of HMS *Highflyer*, who often called at Zanzibar on patrol work and very possibly dined at Captain Fraser's table. According to some accounts the British Consul's wife, Emily Seward, and the young consulate surgeon, Dr John Kirk, were behind the plot – they wished to rid the European trading community of a potentially damaging embarrassment. It was arranged that the princess would take advantage of a religious festival requiring Muslims to go down to the sea and wash, and Captain Pasley would dispatch a cutter to the agreed spot. The princess, who had sold most of her possessions, boarded the cutter with two boxes of dollars and a bag of Zanzibar sand. Several months later Ruete joined her in Aden, where they were married before heading for Hamburg. She changed her name to Emily and became a Lutheran.

The affair, which became known to Majid when one of the princess's servants screamed the news through the streets, caused much alarm among Europeans in Zanzibar. In Majid's eyes Captain Pasley was even more of a villain than Reute. There were fears that reprisals would follow. The British consul, Dr Edward Seward, asked the naval authorities for a ship to be permanently stationed at Zanzibar during the coming months. He warned that the annual invasion of the island by thousands of armed Arab pirates from the north would be worse than usual because of the *Highflyer* incident and 'retaliation upon the virtually defenceless English (sic) and British Indian population would be both easy and inviting.' The ship arrived in the harbour, Majid decided to accept the British consul's assurance that he had known nothing of the plot, and the crisis passed without bloodshed.[14]

Christie said nothing of the affair in his letters home, but possibly his views were not quite the standard British ones. Certainly he was no admirer either of John Kirk, with whom he would clash later, or of

Captain Pasley. The *Highflyer* had salvaged an American cargo ship which had been wrecked nearby and Christie was disgusted with the captain for demanding as a reward 50 per cent of the value of the goods on board, including the items which had not been recovered.

Christie's relationship with Majid was obviously unscathed by the incident, and in the following year he accepted an invitation to spend a week aboard the Sultan's steamer, *Sea King*, while enjoying hippopotamus-shooting on the mainland. The shooting, he recounted to his brother, offered good sport but his account makes it obvious that what he really enjoyed was exploring the hinterland. 'I was out every day from morning till night,' he wrote, 'going up the rivers, along the coast in boats and as far inland as a day's journey.' With two companions he set off on horseback one day for the interior, but after six miles the paths became so narrow that they had to dismount and walk. A guard of five coastal soldiers accompanied them – 'about as wild-looking a lot as you ever saw, armed with matchlocks and crooked daggers, which I am happy to say were not required'. Christie, displaying the curiosity and temperament of an explorer, added that he had been in several places where no European had been before – 'and altogether had a very pleasant time'.[15]

He was enjoying Zanzibar. His health remained good and his medical practice was going well. 'I am succeeding quite as well as I expected in my practice and I can have but little difficulty in making a good living here,' he wrote a year after leaving Scotland. A little later he gave an equally upbeat report: 'I like Zanzibar very much and I shall remain as long as I can. I can get a very comfortable living without much work.'[16]

He seemed to have settled into his new life very well. But, for Christie, this was almost a sign that things were about to change. Here and there in his letters there had been a hint of growing interest in business and of the opportunities that Zanzibar offered to someone who knew both the market and the language. He enormously admired the commercial acumen of the Banyan Indians who made up the bulk of his practice. Attracted by the idea of doing a little business himself he promised to send Andrew, his ironmonger brother, 'information concerning the goods sold here in your line' and added: 'Something in the way of business may be done in odd times.' Undoubtedly he was also influenced by Captain Fraser, fellow-Scot and proprietor of the only British business in Zanzibar, with a soap and oil business in Zanzibar town as well as a large sugar plantation and factory in the north of the island. In the spring of 1867, some 18 months after his arrival in Zanzibar, he announced to his brother: 'I have given up attention to private practice and have entered into a new engagement with Captain Fraser.'[17]

CHAPTER 8
The Sugar Factory

CAPTAIN HUGH ALEXANDER FRASER, the only British businessman on the island, was known to all the westerners in Zanzibar. The name brought groans of dread and dismay in some quarters, for often it spelled trouble. Fraser was a great stirrer of controversy, a mischief-maker and a lover of intrigue, a compulsive and skillful letter-writer with a pen dipped in acid. The consular files in Zanzibar State Archives bulge with letters from, to, and about him. Almost from the moment of his arrival in Zanzibar in 1864 he had made enemies in the British consulate. He accused the consul, Colonel Playfair of the Indian Army, of being guilty of spreading 'a wanton and malicious falsehood' because he had told people that Fraser, who was about to leave for a visit to Britain, was being recalled by the London branch of his firm. Refusing to accept Playfair's disclaimers Fraser insisted that he had been 'systematically subjected to a series of official insults and injustices from you whose duty it was to afford all reasonable countenance and support'.[1] This set the tone for Fraser's future relations with a succession of consular officials.

Fraser was an example, albeit exaggerated, of a familiar type. He has been described as 'one of those Europeans who were to be found often enough in the nineteenth century pursuing a dubious livelihood in out-of-the-way corners of the tropical world'.[2] Epithets like 'rascal', 'rogue' and 'rather a bad hat' were flung at him both in his lifetime and later. Yet he attracted warm admiration in high places. Sir Bartle

Frere, the renowned Governor of Bombay in the 1860s, who had known Fraser in India, described him as 'an old acquaintance and much trusted for his outspoken frankness'; later H.M. Stanley, arriving in Zanzibar to prepare for his search for Livingstone, called him 'one of the sturdiest of Scotsmen, a most pleasant-mannered and unaffected man, sincere and unaffected in whatever he did'.[3] Bishop Tozer and Dr Edward Steere of the Universities Mission were also well disposed towards Fraser, who through his London business associates had transferred money for them without charging for his services. Livingstone, too, arranged for money to be transmitted from London to Captain Fraser so that it would be available for the payment of wages and goods. And once, at a time of gnawing hunger, he 'filled the pot with a first-rate rifle given me by Captain Fraser'.[4]

Christie, too, had obviously thought him trustworthy or he would hardly have given up a successful practice and pleasant life in order to work with him. It seems remarkable that this favourable opinion had survived eight months of life in the Fraser household, with its continual round of commotions and crises. During Christie's stay the house was robbed more than once, the cook was attacked in the street, and there was even a shooting: a member of the household, Fraser's business colleague Edward Bishop, was sitting on the roof terrace one evening when a bullet whizzed past him. Fraser reported the incident to the consulate but received limited sympathy from Dr Edward Seward, who had become acting consul because of Playfair's ill-health. 'Bullets,' Seward wrote in his reply, 'have within my own experience flown very unpleasantly about the Consulate.'[5]

Restless as always and with a thirst for new experiences that Zanzibar had not quenched, Christie was evidently convinced by Fraser's plausible account of the bright prospects for the business. It was certainly ambitious, and at the outset had boasted impressive backers. Fraser had made valuable friends in India. His naval career had allowed him to tap into an influential circle of shipping interests with Clydeside connections. The Indian Navy (or Bombay Marine) had been responsible not only for maritime defence but also for mail and transport services for the imperial government in Bombay. When the navy was disbanded in 1863 in order to save money and encourage private shipping, Fraser was well placed to pursue a profitable career in civilian life. He was set on his path by the brothers John and James Nicol Fleming, sons of a former Lord Provost of Glasgow (James Fleming of Claremont) and partners in W. Nicol & Co., one of Bombay's leading merchant houses. The company, founded by the Flemings' uncle, the Aberdeenshire surgeon William Nicol, was part of the maritime empire of Sir William Mackinnon, who was a close friend of the Flemings. Some people within the Mackinnon group – a web of shipping companies, trading partners and subsidiary firms – thought the Flemings 'fast folks' in their business dealings, and their careers were to end in disgrace because of their role in the City of Glasgow Bank failure; but in the 1860s Nicol & Co. were regarded as a respectable enterprise.[6]

The Flemings for their part regarded Fraser as worthy to be their agent in Zanzibar – and local agent also of John Fleming's London merchant house, Smith, Fleming & Co. They went further and provided him with £70,000 to set up a business on the island.[7] This was no quixotic gesture. With steamships rapidly overtaking sail, there was growing interest in the possibility of establishing regular steamship services between India and East Africa. Nicol & Co. were agents to Sir William Mackinnon's new British India Steam Navigation Co., and Mackinnon was strongly influenced by his close friend Sir Bartle Frere, Governor of Bombay, who believed that subsidised shipping lines could be used as an instrument of foreign policy and in particular as a deterrent to the Indian Ocean slave trade. (Frere himself had been influenced by David Livingstone, who had twice stayed with him in Bombay on his way to and from Africa.)[8]

With an agent in Zanzibar, Nicol & Co. were well positioned to advance these aims – and Fraser was well placed to advance his own considerable ambitions. Or so it seemed. He arrived at Zanzibar in 1864 – evidently unaccompanied by any family although he was married and had at least three daughters. He quickly turned himself into H.A. Fraser & Co. and started an oil and soap factory in the town. Not satisfied with that he purchased about 2400 acres of swampland near Mkokotoni, 20 miles north of Zanzibar town, and began to grow sugar cane as well as coconut palms and various fruits, such as oranges, limes and mangoes. He built drains and roads, an expensively equipped sugar factory and mill, and a house for himself on a hilltop with fine views of the island of Tumbatu.[9]

'The view from the house at Mkokotoni is certainly one of the finest marine views I have seen,' Christie wrote home to Kilmarnock. As doctor to the workforce he was already familiar with the place before beginning his new work there. Soon after his arrival in Zanzibar he had spent several weeks settling his patients into a new hospital on the estate. It can seldom have been short of patients for Captain Fraser's estate rivalled the Universities Mission for poor health and high mortality. The leaders of the Mission were acutely aware of this similarity. They pointed out that their own members were vulnerable to disease simply because they stayed on the island for longer than most Europeans whereas, according to Dr Edward Steere of the Mission, the Mkokotoni deaths were nearly all 'directly attributable to accident or intemperance.'[10] John Kirk, the British Consulate surgeon and future Consul-General, took an equally grim view. 'All their artisans and head men are carried off,' he wrote in a letter. 'They cannot stand it much longer I think.'[11] As far as intemperance was concerned, he indicated, Fraser himself was setting the pace.

But Christie now had more than medical problems on his mind. His new managerial role was a formidable challenge. No sooner had he joined the company than Fraser departed on what would turn out to be extremely extended leave. He gave Christie power of attorney and left him in total charge. Nothing in Christie's experience had equipped him for the management of a large tropical estate and sugar factory and he was not temperamentally suited to the job. He wrote in some alarm to Andrew:

> Well, it is a very large affair to look after and the keeping up and the cash will be no small matter to me – particularly as I have not a very good business head. I shall have first a very large manufacturing and partly mercantile business to manage. Weights, measures, monies, customs etc being all

different from what prevails at home, and in addition to this a foreign language, and worse still a burning climate, God only knows how I can get through it.[12]

Zanzibar's multiple currencies can't have helped his battles with the accounts. Christie's head must have been spinning after a day spent juggling with silver Maria Theresa dollars (first minted in 1780 and popular in East Africa as jewellery as well as currency), American dollars, rupees and pounds sterling.

He could hardly have chosen a worse time to launch himself into his new career. Things had not been going well on the Mkokotoni estate. Five months before Christie took over the management, Nicol & Co. had pulled out of the enterprise. Fraser paid about £40,000 to buy his partner's share of the business, resulting in an urgent need for economies. Christie believed that Nicol had withdrawn from the venture partly because of the dire state of health of the workforce, but there were other reasons. By 1867 Mackinnon and his associates were having second thoughts about establishing a Bombay-to-Zanzibar steamship service. With Zanzibar's export trade largely in American hands, such a line would not be very remunerative. Nicol & Co. sent a pessimistic assessment to the Chief Secretary of Government in Bombay.[13]

There must also have been second thoughts about Fraser himself. His use of slave labour on the plantation was a source of embarrassment to his backers and indeed to the British anti-slave movement. Obtaining free labour in a slave economy was difficult, and as a British subject Fraser was forbidden by an Act of 1843 from purchasing slaves. He solved the difficulty by hiring them. Since Zanzibar was an independent state rather than an imperial outpost there was no legal barrier to their use, only – for British subjects – to their purchase. Fraser drew up contracts with four Arab slave owners for the supply of 500 slaves (more were negotiated later). The owners were to be paid 'on delivery' a year's wages for each slave at the rate of $2 per month, which added up to approximately the market price for slaves. In subsequent years Fraser was to pay each slave a wage of half a dollar per month, with nothing going to the owners. At the end of five years the slaves would be freed.[14]

'Captain Fraser is going in for slave labour on a large scale,' commented David Livingstone disapprovingly.[15] Christie suspected that Livingstone had stirred up the row that soon blazed over this issue. Livingstone's old enemy, Bishop Tozer, was more sympathetic since Fraser had readily agreed that the slaves should be given religious instruction by the Universities Mission. There was little sympathy for Fraser, however, at the British consulate. Dr Edward Seward, the acting consul, believed that the deal amounted to an illegal purchase because all property in the slaves was virtually transferred to Fraser. This, he added, should not be concealed by 'a veil of philanthropy'. In letters to his superiors in Bombay and the Foreign Office he argued that British anti-slavery measures in the Indian Ocean would look nonsensical if Zanzibar were to be made into a 'sugar island' by a British firm using slave labour; and to the Arabs 'the riddle would be incomprehensible'.[16]

The Foreign Secretary, Lord Stanley, took Seward's comments seriously enough to submit the contract to the law officers. Fraser was furious when he found out. He had not been told of this development but happened to hear about it on the rumour mill when he was visiting one of the British naval ships in Zanzibar harbour (probably HMS *Wasp*, whose captain was Norman Bedingfeld, Livingstone's detested second-in-command during the Zambezi expedition). He wrote to Seward, saying that he had 'reason to believe that a sinister influence has been exerted to press the present case against me' and identifying the consulate as the almost-certain source of the remarks that he had heard when aboard the ship. This, he added, 'unmistakably suggests the key to the whole proceedings against me'. He enclosed what he hoped would be his trump card: – the copy of a slightly earlier but very similar contract drawn up for him by the then British consul, Colonel Playfair, who had urged him to adopt it.[17]

Legal proceedings would probably have been taken against Fraser if Seward, with every reason to wish to avoid the embarrassment that this would bring to the consulate, had not found a way out. Since the law lords had ruled that Fraser's slaves would remain slaves until their emancipation, Seward persuaded the Sultan to emancipate them immediately. At a stroke some 700 men and women were transformed from slaves to free labourers, and work at the plantation continued as before.[18]

That was how matters stood when Christie took up his new post in the early spring of 1867, but because communications with London were still so slow it was not until the summer that a letter was received from the Foreign Secretary, who declared that since the matter was this 'happily settled' no proceedings would be taken against Fraser & Co. All that remained was for the Foreign Office to express its gratitude by presenting Majid with a portrait of Queen Victoria – except that they had to think again when the Queen declined to sit for the Sultan.[19]

That should have been the end of the matter but Fraser, spending time in London during his extended leave, was still fuming. He and his London partner, John Fleming, were given an interview at the Foreign Office and afterwards, still determined to embarrass Seward, he sent his interviewers his copy of the original contract endorsed by Colonel Playfair. The Foreign Office sought an opinion from a firm of Temple Bar lawyers, who ruled that although the contract itself was not illegal, the transfer of slaves was. Fraser had no ammunition left.[20]

A proviso to Lord Stanley's promise not to enforce any penalties was that Fraser & Co. should 'undertake on their part to abstain in the future from all similar offences'. With Fraser still out of the country it fell to Christie to give the promise and in December, 1867 he dutifully wrote to the new British consul, H.A. Churchill, promising that 'we will abstain in future from entering into such contracts.'[21]

By this time, not surprisingly, Christie was thoroughly disenchanted with the Mkokotoni estate. 'I have no intention of maintaining any connection with the business here longer than Captain Fraser's return from England,' he had written to his brother in the early summer of 1867, only about three months after taking up his new position. Reluctantly he settled down to manage the estate in the meantime, turning down an invitation to join a distinguished Scottish medical practice in Bombay because he felt unable to adapt to the routine. But it was to be a long wait for Fraser's return.

There were compensations, however. Christie was pleased at the change that Fraser's absence brought about in the lifestyle of his circle. As he told Andrew: 'We now keep very little company, and I for one never go out visiting. I spend my time at home and merely make a few necessary calls. Keeping open house as we did was both highly injurious to the pocket and to the head . . . I am tired . . . of meeting the officers and I intend to steer clear of them.'

He was becoming aware that Fraser was not the world's best businessman. 'I cannot say how business is likely to turn out here, the current expenses being enormous,' he confessed to Andrew, adding that a profitable business could be run with home partners who really understood the trade. Even the successful transformation of the Mkokotoni slaves into a free labour force did not thrill him, although unlike Fraser he believed that the East African slave trave must be brought to an end. The newly freed slaves, bemused by this sudden change in their lives, seemed to hanker after the certainties of their former stature. Chatting to the African in charge of the large engine at the sugar factory Christie was interested to learn that the man had had plenty to eat before and 'did not understand about this freedom'.[22]

Captain Fraser's leave lasted for more than a year and it was not until the summer of 1868 that Christie wrote to Kilmarnock that his engagement had terminated. Restless again, he considered what to do next. He thought he might enter the Sultan's service but also had 'some thoughts' of going into the interior from Mombasa to the lake district, a journey which had not yet been made by any European. In the end he was persuaded by the Captain to keep up a connection with Mkokotoni, so the final break did not come for another year.

At last, in July, 1869, he wrote to Andrew: 'I have no connection with the concern except in my medical capacity and since the beginning of this month have resumed my medical practice, which at present promises fairly. I regret much now that I did not stick to it alone from the first, but I was beguiled by better prospects which did not turn out as I expected.'[23]

He did well to pull out of an increasingly shaky enterprise. At first Captain Fraser won plaudits for his exemplary management of a paid workforce – a novelty in that part of the world. Mkokotoni came to be regarded as a model for the future, showing that the agricultural development of Zanzibar could be carried on without slaves. Sir Bartle Frere, visiting the plantation while on a diplomatic mission to Zanzibar in 1873, remarked that Fraser had 'in some respect almost unconsciously' removed some of the obstacles to the total abolition of the slave trade. This was ironic, since Fraser himself continued to agitate against abolition on the grounds that it would destroy British commercial interests in East Africa.

Unfortunately the model estate was hardly a model of good management. Sinking into debt, Fraser sold the estate to an Indian entrepreneur and rented it back. When a shipping line between Zanzibar and Aden was finally established in 1871 he was made its local agent but was soon replaced. He fraudulently evaded his commitments to his creditors and finally, in late 1874, was declared bankrupt. Without warning he made an escape from Zanzibar almost as dramatic as Princess Salme's had been, sailing for Natal with a huge cargo of sugar which rightly belonged to his creditors. He is then said to have headed off for the goldfields of the Transvaal.

But that was still five years in the future in the summer of 1869 when Christie, older and wiser, waved goodbye to a disastrous entrepreneurial career. His return to his former trade turned out to be a good thing not only for his pocket but for medical science – though it was only just in time.

CHAPTER 9
Betsy

CHRISTIE was in low spirits as he approached his fortieth birthday in May, 1869. He was then in the final few months of his engagement at the sugar factory. His disenchantment with the business, and disappointment at his failure to profit from it, had begun to colour his outlook on Zanzibar. 'Had one the prospect of realising a fortune in a short time it would be all very well,' he wrote to his brother. 'But I am not and never will be a fortune maker.'

He was upset when the Glaswegian manager of the sugar plantation, Gibson, began to drink heavily – or, in Christie's words, 'has gone all to the devil here . . . having seldom been sober since he came here'. The British Consul appointed a commission to report on whether 'the full use of his liberty could be entrusted to him' and Christie as one of its members felt bound to report to the contrary. This was upsetting for him. Gibson had been a friend. Christie had thought well of him to begin with – 'a fine gentleman' – and was pleased when his brother Andrew visited him during his leave in Glasgow. But now, after the commission's report, Christie felt that there could be no more communication with his former friend. Embarrassingly, Gibson's sister was about to arrive from Glasgow for a visit and it looked as if she would have to head for home again with her brother almost immediately on arrival.[1]

Christie's mood seemed to be lifted by an invitation to join Sultan Majid's party in another hippo-shooting expedition on the mainland.

Although he took several shots at the animals he seemed not quite at home with this unfortunate sport and found it 'rather alarming when a herd of them rise close to your small boat'. However, there was some additional entertainment on this trip. It was Ramadan, which closed with a great festival in which the coastal chiefs came to pay their respects to the Sultan and perform a ritual dance for him. Christie was sufficiently cheered to joke to his brother that he might start a group called Christie's Minstrels 'to restore my fallen fortunes'.[2]

The mood didn't last. In the spring of 1869 Christie suffered an attack of fever followed alarmingly by partial paralysis of the extremities. He soon recovered sufficiently to undertake a day's journey from Mombasa into the interior to spend a few days at the Wesleyan mission station, but on his return to Zanzibar the fever recurred, accompanied by vomiting and weakness. He was scarcely able to crawl about. From his bed he heard firing at sea as a British naval ship attacked a slave dhow, but didn't get up 'as my innards are being torn up by dreadful vomiting'.

In a mood of despair he wrote to Andrew: 'I am tired . . . I am sick.' He made up his mind to leave Zanzibar as soon as possible and asked his brother to look out for a suitable post for him at home – preferably something 'small and quiet and out of the way'. He was convinced that two or three more attacks of fever would finish him or leave him an invalid for life. And he did have another attack, early in May. 'I really thought it was all up with me,' he wrote to Andrew afterwards.[3]

Illness seemed to make him bad tempered. There was a testy note in his letters.

His health improved somewhat after the bout of fever in early May, and he decided to remain in Zanzibar for a little longer. But he remained in ill humour, judging by the tone of a letter to Andrew. 'You people,' he wrote, 'never seem to think that one out here is living in a kind of oven by day and by night, and writing a long letter is no joke.'

His life still did not run smoothly. There was a depressing development on the diplomatic front. The British Consul, H.A. Churchill, who had been almost constantly ill since his arrival from

Bombay two years earlier, finally went on extended sick leave in June, 1869. John Kirk, the talented and ambitious consulate surgeon, became acting consul and acting political agent to Bombay – another rung on his ladder to diplomatic fame. 'I do not like the change,' wrote Christie to Andrew.[4]

Kirk, a son of the manse, was three years older than Christie and a graduate of Edinburgh University in both botany and medicine. He had served as botanist with Livingstone on the Zambezi expedition and had been in effect second-in-command. Unlike most British members of the expedition he had not fallen out permanently with his leader. Livingstone had soon afterwards tried to use his influence with Sir Bartle Frere, Governor of Bombay, to have Kirk appointed Consul in Zanzibar, and when the move failed because of Kirk's inexperience he pushed to have him made agency surgeon. The appointment was in the Governor's gift because of the dual nature of consular posts in Zanzibar (even the choice of consul was largely left to Bombay although the appointment was formally made by the Foreign Office). Normally a doctor in British India would have been chosen to fill the minor post of agency surgeon, but after hearing Livingstone's pleas Frere said: 'That decided it.' Kirk was immediately appointed, arriving in Zanzibar at about the same time as Christie.[5]

Christie's view of Kirk was very different from Livingstone's. He seethed with animosity towards his fellow-Scot and fellow-doctor. He was far from alone in being antagonised by Kirk's assertive personality, but in addition there may have been ill-feeling between the two doctors over their respective relations with Sultan Majid. The Sultan seemed to take an instant liking to Christie, invited him on expeditions, made him physician to his army and navy, and asked him to treat his sick relatives (although when he himself was ill he would let no European near him); but his relations with Kirk were less cordial.

Christie's dislike of Kirk was amply reciprocated. The two men clashed soon after Kirk had taken up his appoinment as acting consul. Kirk tried Christie in the consular court on a charge of tying up and imprisoning a man. He found him guilty and imposed a fine. Christie, however, had received no summons, was tried in his absence, and –

according to his own account – knew nothing about the trial until afterwards. He refused to pay the fine. Kirk threatened him with a new trial, which would probably result in imprisonment as well as a fine. Christie said that he would refuse to appear and that he intended to bring the case to the attention of the Foreign Office.[6] At that point the affair appears to have been defused. There are no further references to it in Christie's letters, and certainly he did not go to jail.

Amid these difficulties Christie felt isolated from his friends at home. In April, 1869, he noted that he had not received a letter for more than a year. 'I feel as if I were for ever cut off from the civilised world,' he wrote. This was the result of haphazard postal arrangements rather than neglect. Zanzibar was the main entrepot of East Africa but the Indian Ocean remained a backwater as far as much of the world was concerned. There were no regular shipping lines, no mail steamers. Christie's letters were carried to and from Scotland by obliging naval or merchant officers. The Suez Canal, which would bring Zanzibar some 2000 sea miles nearer European ports and make regular shipping services a more attractive proposition, would not open till the end of that year. Until then, and for some time afterwards, British contacts with East Africa were far slighter than those with West Africa. There was no post office in Zanzibar in Christie's day, and a telegraph cable would not be landed until several years after he had left the island.

There was a more specific source of his loneliness. About a year after Christie's arrival in Zanzibar his brother Andrew had married Sarah Robb, a farmer's daughter whom he had met at Cumnock flower show. In the summer of 1867 a daughter was born. Christie sent presents to his new niece and remarked that Andrew had 'got ahead of me now' but that he would make up on him 'in due course'. Abruptly he added: 'Do you know of any likely female to send out? – Mrs C. may do so. Young smart female for wife.'[7]

He returned to the subject early in 1869, the approach to his landmark birthday making him conscious no doubt of the passing of time. 'I thought I would have been married by this time myself, but all my prospects seem to fail, and there is no pick and choose here,' he wrote. I wish much that I had brought out a wife with me as I would have been much more comfortable and richer than I am now.'[8]

Six months later he made a startling announcement. 'Since my last letter to you I have received a consignment of a wife,' he wrote to Andrew. She was Betsy Kidd, aged 32, the daughter of the keeper of Edzell Castle in Angus (his duties were to look after this much admired ruin and show visitors round).[9] How the marriage was arranged – and whether the couple had even met before – remains a mystery. There was no obvious point of contact between the Kidds and the Christies (although Betsy Kidd's brother was in the same trade as James Christie's late father). Certainly Andrew had never seen his brother's bride, for Christie remarked in his letter that sending photographs would be 'better than saying anything about the original' and he expected the arrival of a photographer from the Seychelles soon. His own photograph, he added, might interest Andrew for he was 'greatly altered' and had a beard and a moustache.

There were difficulties in arranging the marriage 'as all the authorities declared they had no power, and Betsy Kidd spent more than three weeks as the guest of Miss Gibson, the visiting sister of the inebriated manager from Glasgow. Eventually the wedding took place in the British consulate's mission chapel, with Bishop Tozer performing the ceremony. 'We had a rather stylish breakfast,' Christie reported to Andrew. All the European consuls were there and a letter of congratulations arrived from the Sultan, who was on the mainland.[10]

The couple occupied the Moorish-style waterfront house that Christie had rented for several years. Their cook was a former slave boy, Frajella, who supplemented his cooking skills by learning to assist his master at surgical operations. The household also included Christie's grey parrot, which used to 'hawk and spit like a native every morning', possibly not to the delight of the new Mrs Christie. With as many patients as he could cope with, Christie's medical practice, which he had resumed around the time of his marriage, was building up rapidly. 'I cannot say that I am in the way of realising a fortune, but I am quite comfortable,' he told Andrew. His health had improved greatly and within a few weeks of the wedding he was reporting to his brother that married life suited him well, although he described its advantages in ungallant terms. Living alone in Zanzibar had been 'exceedingly uncomfortable and very expensive' but these disadvantages were, he found, much decreased by 'the double mode of life'.

What he didn't know at this stage was that doubts about the validity of the marriage had arisen in official minds. It was not until more than a year had passed that the consulate received a sharp communication from the Foreign Office which stated that John Kirk, as acting consul, had arranged for a marriage certificate under the provisions of a Government of India Act instead of the relevant Westminster Act. This was probably because his position had never been officially recognised by the Foreign Office, only by the Bombay Government. The unfortunate H.A. Churchill, who was obviously feeling too ill to think of such things when he handed over control to Kirk before going on sick leave, was reprimanded for not having obtained the Foreign Secretary's formal recognition of Kirk's status as acting consul. Bishop Tozer, too, was drawn into the controversy: he felt moved to protest to the Foreign Secretary, Lord Clarendon, after receiving a letter from the Bombay Government's solicitor which questioned the legality of the marriage and 'appeared to reflect on the conduct of the Acting Political Resident and myself'.

After a considerable flurry of correspondence the problem was solved by a Parliamentary Bill for legalising various marriages 'irregularly solemnised abroad'. The Government agreed to Tozer's suggestion that a consular official should be permanently authorised to register marriages in the absence of the consul.[11]

In the meantime the 'dual mode of life' had become rather less comfortable. The 1869 cholera epidemic, the most severe ever suffered by Zanzibar, reached the island six months after the Christies' marriage. Afterwards Christie was to remark that he could not have coped with the terrible burden of his work at this time if he had still been single.

CHAPTER 10
Cholera

THE CLOSING MONTHS of 1869 in Zanzibar were unusually dry for that time of year. October was pleasant and moderately cool. The north-east monsoon set in early but brought only light rains. There was none of the usual sickness associated with the rainy season – no diarrhoea or similar disorders. Christie had never seen the town so free from disease. In the early part of November he had no patients on his sick list except for a few surgical cases. 'There was nothing for a medical man to do,' he recalled later.[1]

But ominous reports were circulating. A caravan arriving in the mainland port of Pangani, diagonally opposite Zanzibar, brought news of a dreadful plague raging in the interior. It was evident from the descriptions that the disease was cholera. John Kirk, at the British consulate, reported the news to the Bombay Government. It would have been received with no great surprise. Cholera, for long confined to its natural habitat in the Ganges Delta, had broken free in 1817 by latching on in particularly virulent form to Indian troops on the march between Madras and the Ganges Delta. The scene was set for the great nineteenth-century cholera pandemics. The new steel-hulled steamships and the trade radiating out from the Raj were among developments ensuring that each wave would travel faster and further than the previous one, reaching as far as North America by the 1830s. Zanzibar narrowly escaped the first pandemic but not the second, which had struck the island in 1836, and the third, in the 1850s. The next pandemic had been averted by a slightly out-of-season monsoon in 1865, but now cholera was heading unstoppably in Zanzibar's direction.

Zanzibar's rulers appeared unconcerned. As Christie put it, 'Not a single precautionary step was taken to secure the population of the town and island against the impending invasion.' Before the end of October news arrived that the epidemic had reached Pangani itself, but still the reaction in Zanzibar was passive. The Arab authorities were fatalistic. They saw no need for preventive measures or medical contingency plans. There was no question of imposing a quarantine or of preventing dhows from Pangani landing their cargo at Zanzibar. John Kirk argued in favour of an effort to remove some of the 'accumulation of filth that spreads the disease' but the dirt simply renewed itself from day to day.[2] His masters in Bombay were not much help.

The first cholera case in Zanzibar was at Mangapwani, one of the villages where the dhows from Pangani often anchored for the night, sometimes letting off passengers who walked the 10 miles to the town. A death from cholera was reported the day after passengers were known to have landed there. Soon reports of sudden deaths among Africans were circulating in the town. Some became ill at work and staggered home to die; others collapsed in the street.[3] Christie thought at first that the cause was probably sunstroke. December and January were the hottest months he had ever known in Zanzibar – 'the sky was like a dome of polished steel, and the rays of the sun scorched and blistered.' Coolies and porters could be seen staggering along the streets under burdens that might have taxed horses. Others worked in ill-ventilated sheds. Heatstroke would hardly have been surprising.[4]

But soon there could be no doubt that cholera had arrived. An outbreak of epidemic proportions flared up among the slave population in the Melinde quarter at the north-west end of Zanzibar town – a densely packed district containing the salt market, goat's meat butcheries and the shark bazaar. Its centre was crammed with the houses of the poorer Arabs, who worked as mat-makers, butchers, soldiers and often, when no better work was to be had, as porters alongside the Africans. Christie, who noted that not all cholera cases developed into epidemic centres, identified the house of an Arab slaveholder as 'the spark among the combustibles' that had ignited this outbreak of uncontrollable fury. The man employed porters who loaded and discharged vessels at Mangapwani, where dhows from the mainland landed passengers. Christie realised that a single case could be enough to 'poison the life fountains of an entire community' when it found the right material around it. As the filthiest quarter in town Melinde offered ideal conditions with its maze of overcrowded streets and its mass of African huts thatched with coconut leaves. The huts, devoid of light and ventilation, fringed a beach of sewage mud on which an ancient deposit of dungheaps was solid enough to withstand even the spring tides.

At first the epidemic was confined to Africans. Christie, whose only African patients were surgical cases, began to think that the epidemic would be over before he had a chance to see the disease. He decided to take the initiative. He asked some of his Arab neighbours to send for him when one of their slaves became ill, and his own servants were also asked to alert him. But the Arabs told him that their slaves died so quickly that this was impossible, and November was almost over before Christie saw his first case.

An Arab neighbour asked him to attend a young Abyssinian servant, 'a remarkably handsome woman', who had been suddenly seized with vertigo. There had been no diarrhoea, nausea, cramps or any of the other symptoms most often associated with cholera. Christie examined her carefully and found no tenderness or pain, no coldness of the extremities – 'only a certain wildness of the eyes, a restlessness of manner, and an anxious aspect of countenance'. Although her pulse quivered and her heart beat rapidly Christie tried to tell her that she might recover, but she turned to her master and said, 'Oh, my master, I am dying' and threw herself down upon the cushions on the floor. Within a quarter of an hour her wrists were pulseless, a cold claminess had crept over her, her voice became hollow and sepulchral and her eyes sunken, and nothing but cold water could relieve her burning thirst. She was dead within four hours of the first recognition of symptoms.[5]

From then on he was not short of patients. Although the disease had originally been confined to Africans this soon changed. By December the entire population of Melinde was affected, Arabs as well as African slaves. In Christie's words 'there was neither house nor hut into which death did not enter.' At first Africans could be seen hurrying to the various burial places on the outskirts of the town, with dead bodies fastened in a piece of matting and lashed to a pole; but eventually, in the intense heat, the effort to scoop out shallow graves became too much and bodies were abandoned on the beach or thrown over the bridge into the sea. As Melinde was the main labour market, normal life in the town soon became impossible – there were no porters to be had, no day labourers.

Soon cholera also reached out to other districts in town and to distant parts of the island. Once Christie walked past part of the suburbs used for burials and saw the entire space 'red like a newly ploughed field' with bones and skulls scattered on the ground and rotting remains lying in the bush. The stench was sickening.

Christie was apprehensive when the start of Ramadan on December 6 was signalled by the appearance of the thin crescent of the new moon. In his ears the boom of the cannons welcoming the holy month sounded like the death knell of thousands. He told several leading men of different Muslim sects that a month of strict dawn-to-dusk fasting would increase vulnerability to the disease, but they replied that a month of special prayer was the best means of averting the pestilence, and that if death did come they would accept their fate and die in the observance of their religious duties.

Christie's fears were quickly realised. The terrible sights reminded him of a beleaguered city whose inhabitants were 'daily falling in hundreds under the rifles of an unseen foe'. Until Ramadan the epidemic had scarcely affected the Khojahs – the Muslim Indians – but now it attacked them in full force, spreading from one branch of a family to another, frequently in another part of the town. By night and day the Khojahs could be seen hurrying to the houses of stricken relatives to give what help they could, in accordance with their custom. Arriving at the house of a patient Christie would find the sick chamber crowded to suffocation. 'I generally had to give a distinct order to keep the room clear, while I was present, as breathing would have been otherwise impossible,' he recalled later. After spending several hours with a sick relative the visitors would head for their own homes and families, bearing with them, in Christie's words, 'the germs of the deadly disease under which they themselves soon fell victims'. The survivors spent all their time looking after the sick and burying the dead, and before long almost all business was suspended. Nearly all the shops closed, apart from a few selling basic necessities.[6]

Zanzibar had become a strange, silent place. People sat passively at their shop doors. The only passers-by were small groups hurrying silently along to help sick relatives. Children's laughter was no longer heard. Africans no longer gathered on the beach on moonlit nights to listen to the music of the tom-tom. 'Even in the death-chamber,' Christie noted, 'there were no frantic demonstrations of grief, no tearing of hair and rending of clothes; but only a natural expression of grief, common to all, when ties of the closest nature were severed for ever; tears were hidden and sobs suppressed or only given vent to in private'. Although the sun shone brightly and the sky was clear the silence of death pervaded the city. The only sounds were those associated with death. As Christie described it:

> When the plague was at its very height, raging in every quarter of the city like a devouring element, threatening all with destruction, praying parties, and Koranic chanters were organised, and they perambulated the streets by night, invoking God to stay the pestilence, and spare the living. Sounds of prayer and solemn Amens issued from the mosques, and from private houses in the streets, and in the early morning the call of the Muzzein to prayers sounded over the city.[7]

Even funerals were muted. There were no sounds of grief, no hired keeners. 'Everything connected with the Muslim funeral is plain, simple and appropriate, and forms a striking and pleasing contrast to the ostentatious and vulgar displays of Christendom,' noted Christie, who was in many respects an atypical Victorian.

This strange passivity set the Zanzibar outbreak apart from many cholera epidemics elsewhere. There was no panic, no headlong flight to the countryside, no unrest or rebellion against authority, no tendency to neglect the sick. Christie was full of admiration for the way the main victims of the epidemic – Zanzibar's Muslim population of Arabs, Khojan Indians, and Africans – acquitted themselves 'in the unequal struggle with death'. Several of the wealthier Arabs took the precaution of staying at home – but that was all. At the height of the epidemic a gloom spread over the whole town as if all the inhabitants were aware that by nightfall they might be dead.

Christie was impressed by the way that even then the living and healthy accorded to the sick and the dying 'those kindly offices which they themselves might soon require at the hands of others.' The apathetic Arab rulers did not become the object of popular rage. The Muslim Africans, who were the hardest hit by the outbreak, believed, according to Christie, that 'death was inflicted by the hand of the destroying angel, and that the black race was doomed, but the European exempt' – some gave themselves a coat of whitewash to fool the evil spirit.[8]

Western residents did seem immune. But visitors living on ships were a different matter. The harbour, as Christie put it, was steaming with cholera. Entire crews of native craft were lost, and 19 Europeans and Americans died aboard square-rigged ships and other visiting vessels. The start of the epidemic coincided with the 'time of the two sails', the period between the monsoons when sailing in both directions became possible to a limited extent. The harbour was always busy at that time, full of native craft such as the dhow, with its sharp prow and towering square stern. There were no harbour regulations, so the vessels could anchor anywhere. They were so tightly packed that it was difficult for boats to pass between them. Christie noted that these vessels were never cleaned from the day they were launched till their timbers were broken up, so it was not surprising that they became plague spots.[9]

The crews of the western ships soon began to succumb. The stewardess of an American barque, newly arrived from Aden and bound for New York, died after becoming ill on a shore visit, and three crew members died soon afterwards. There were 16 cases and four deaths among the crew of a Portuguese barque, although it was clean and had been fumigated and disinfected. The wife of an American ship's captain also died, and a barque with a British crew lost an elderly man to the disease, although a young man recovered. The stoker, chief engineer and a crew member of a British steamship also died, and Christie noted that the ship had an unhealthy berth opposite the foulest part of the sea beach and that the deck was swarming with Zanzibaris when all hands were busy with coals and cargo. The chief engineer had refused to be admitted to the British government building which Kirk had made available for use as a hospital for the crews of ships.[10]

Some visiting ships hastily put to sea again after taking on provisions, but one American vessel was delayed when a member of the crew deserted. The captain set off in pursuit, spotted the man among some African huts, and gave chase for three miles before collaring him and returning him to the ship. On the same day Christie examined all the crew and was satisfied that no one was seriously ill. Later he learned that the deserter had died at sea a few days later. His symptoms left no room for doubt about the diagnosis.[11]

Among westerners on land there was only one death, possibly from disease imported directly from the interior. The Rev. Lewis Fraser, who had been on a mission to the mainland, landed at Mkokotoni and on a day of burning heat set off to ride the 25 miles to town, stopping to quench his thirst at various streams. Christie happened to see him immediately on his arrival at the Universities Mission. His eyes were bloodshot and he looked on the point of collapse from heat stroke. Next day he became seriously ill, although not at first with classic cholera symptoms. Christie's doubts were removed when the man's body surface became very cold while he complained of a sensation of burning heat and could not be restrained from pouring cold water on his naked body. He died at the mission house a week after his arrival in town. Two of the mission's African boys died at around the same time, and several others died at a later stage of the epidemic, but there were no more cases among the British members of the mission, although Bishop Tozer took plenty of risks. Christie was very impressed by the way he 'attended personally to the stricken, and not only administered the medicines with his own hands, but took into his own room, during the night, sufferers from cholera, lest they be neglected in the hands of others'.[12]

At the height of the epidemic Christie himself never had more than two consecutive hours' rest – to have managed more, he claimed, would have meant going into hiding. Sometimes, when he felt he had to be near a patient for an hour or so during the critical period, he would sit at night under the palm-leaf verandah of the house, with the dead stillness broken only by the sound of footsteps as another body was brought to the nearby bridge to be thrown over into the tide below. He shuddered when he heard, not very far away, wild dogs fighting over the bodies of the dead. Sometimes he began to fear that he himself was succumbing to the disease.[13]

As he moved continuously from patient to patient Christie was very much on his own professionally. There were only two other doctors at work on the island – John Kirk and the French consular surgeon. Amid the fury of the epidemic they would have had little time to confer, although Christie did think it strange that as the one doctor with a large practice he was never consulted by the consulate.

Christie's only guidelines were the notes given to him by his friend John McLatchie, who had been a physician at the temporary fever hospital during the 1848-49 epidemic in Glasgow. McLatchie had recommended the use of creosote, a crude version of carbolic acid which was frowned upon by some physicians because of its toxicity and repellent taste. Christie preferred to administer carbolic acid itself. It was a time when Lister's experiments in antiseptic surgery and Pasteur's germ theory were beginning to converge to produce new approaches to the treatment of infectious and contagious diseases. The idea was that internal antisepsis would rid the digestive tract of cholera fermentation.

Since the Zanzibar epidemic occurred only five years after Lister's groundbreaking use of antiseptic in surgery at Glasgow Royal Infirmary, Christie must have been among the first doctors to treat cholera in this way.[14] He later claimed that his use of carbolic acid was successful enough to warrant further trials, but he offered no facts and figures to back up his claim.

He also experimented with electro-galvanic therapy. This was no novelty even if it is surprising to find it in use in Zanzibar at that time. Medical electricity had been attracting increasing interest in the previous two decades, particularly for the treatment of cholera (a patient had been given electric shock treatment in Scotland during the cholera epidemic of 1832). The electrodes on the galvanic battery were attached to different parts of the patient's anatomy according to the preference of the physician, but Christie has left no record of the details of his treatment.[15] He made no claims for its success, which is not surprising since none of the various nineteenth-century prophylactics worked at all, though patients given opium pills were more fortunate than those given emetics. Collectively the cholera treatments of that time have been described as 'largely a form of benevolent homicide'.[16]

Surprisingly for one so interested in ethnic customs, Christie in his subsequent account of the epidemic made no mention of local therapies or even the lack of them. He did however refer to the Arab custom of massaging the extremities of sick relatives, which he thought could be helpful in some circumstances, and he was aware that Richard Burton had reported the use of opium and *mvinyo* – locally distilled spirits – by Africans on the East African mainland. (Burton considered this treatment benign in comparison with that of Anglo-Indian surgeons who 'murder patients with mercury, the lancet and the chafing dish'.)

The epidemic seemed to have burned itself out by the end of

January, without the assistance of any sanitary or medical intervention by Zanzibar's rulers. Religious services were held by relieved Muslims. The Europeans, too, held a service of thanksgiving. But almost immediately afterwards the disease broke out again with tremendous virulence – first among visitors and then for the second time among inhabitants. Christie called it a double epidemic. In March, April and May his notebook was again filling up with cases of sudden deaths among Africans. In Mkototoni plantation, where he had so recently worked, there were 180 cases on the sick list in early April.

The key was the change in the direction of the monsoon. In early March the dhows began to head off for southern ports while the north-east monsoon still made the voyage possible, and merchants and agents from the northern Somali ports poured in, ready to do business before returning with the south-west monsoon. Along with them came huge numbers of 'tenda hulwas' – heavily armed slave dealers and desperadoes who moved into the Melinde quarter with the intention of kidnapping Africans and shipping them home. Christie realised that these crowds of strangers 'unwittingly dropped in on the smouldering embers of the cholera epidemic'.[17]

By early May the outlook had improved again. The dhows for the north had sailed away with the onset of the south-west monsoon. The desperadoes had all gone home. The cholera count in town was down to a few cases. But suddenly there was a new danger. The beginning of May marked the start of the open season for the importation of slaves to the island. Under a treaty with Britain no slaves could be landed during the north-east monsoon – when it would have been almost impossible to do so in any case, since most of the slave dhows came from the ports to the south of Zanzibar and could hardly have beat up against the monsoon. From May until the south-west monsoon ended at the beginning of January some 20,000 slaves were reckoned to pass every year through the Zanzibar market, the first of them arriving in packed slave dhows on May 3rd or 4th.

This time there was special reason for haste. Cholera had broken out at Kilwa, the principal mainland port from which slaves were shipped to Zanzibar. The slaves were dying every day in their hundreds. Their deaths represented a heavy loss to the Arabs who had a stake in slave caravans, and also to Zanzibar customs officials, who earned two dollars of duty per slave. The dhows were packed with slaves as close as they could stand, some of them suffering from cholera, many of them dying, all of them emaciated in the extreme. The dead were tossed overboard and so were some of the living if they were thought to have become so emaciated that they had lost their market value. No food or water was provided during the passage.[18]

Christie, whose waterfront house was near the customs house, used to watch them land. Once he noticed a naked woman who was apparently unaware that the child in her arms had died, its arms flapping about and its tongue protruding. On another occasion he watched as a dhow came into harbour with some 250 slaves aboard, crouched together 'as closely as people could stand or could be packed'. The dying were left to expire on the sands so that there would be no customs duty to pay, while 'living skeletons' were dragged and kicked along past Christie's door. That evening he and two companions found an exhausted woman staggering along near the outskirts of the town. Bishop Tozer looked after her until her death about two weeks later. It seemed that she had been thrown overboard but the water was shallow so she had been able to wade ashore. She thought that two others had drowned. The case was reported but no investigation followed.

Christie described this as a disgrace to civilisation and added that the case was not at all exceptional. As he described the scene that he witnessed daily from his window:

> Gangs of living skeletons were landed, with death
> imprinted on every feature; full grown men and women as
> naked as at the hour of their birth . . . . Thousands of
> negroes were rushed into Zanzibar in this condition, and
> the most pitiable sights ever witnessed by human eye were
> daily to be seen on the streets in open daylight.[19]

The slaves, far too sick to attract purchasers, were dying at the rate of two hundred a day. 'Human beings,' Christie wrote later, 'were being offered for sale at fifty shillings a dozen, without finding a purchaser.' Speculators then bought them at a cheaper price and rushed them off to the market in the hope that a sufficient number would survive to leave a margin of profit.

The slaves triggered a third wave of the epidemic. Huge numbers of them had cholera when they arrived in Zanzibar. Mortality at Kilwa, their departure-point, was known to be appalling. Zanzibar harbour became infected again and there were isolated cases in town until the middle of July when the disease at last receded.

In a letter to his brother Christie confessed that he could hardly have coped but for Betsy, who always had every comfort ready for him when he got home from his cholera labours. He added a sad note about his finances. 'Perhaps you may think that I made a good thing out of this,' he wrote, 'but I never had the knack of making much money, and I must say that the toil greatly exceeded the profit.'[20]

He gave his brother a brief account of the outbreak, but at this stage did not confess that he himself had been responsible for a case of cholera in his own household: he had returned one day with his clothes 'sodden with discharges' and had neglected to deal with them. The result was a case of cholera the following day, fortunately not fatal, and Christie's wording leaves open the possibility that the invalid was his wife.[21] He was under the impression that this was the only cholera case among Zanzibar's European residents, but in fact John Kirk's infant daughter also caught the disease, and also recovered.[22]

But there were peculiar features of this epidemic which would need to be described to a wider audience than Christie's brother and family. He had not yet finished with cholera.

CHAPTER 11

The Great Highways

WHEN THE EPIDEMIC had retreated Christie tried to assess the damage. This wasn't easy. Not even the size of the population was known: Zanzibar's rulers regarded record-keeping, even at household level, as a violation of the laws of god. Thirteen years earlier the explorer Richard Burton had estimated the urban population at 25,000 but Christie, who was familiar with every corner of town and suburbs, put the number at between 80,000 and 100,000 and thought the population of the whole island must be between 300,000 and 400,000.[1] He calculated the average mortality among Africans by finding out the number of deaths in certain households in different parts of town – and was surprised to find that there had been 30 deaths in a house close to his own, although at the time he had not been aware of more than one.

The smaller slave-holders answered his questions freely. Some had lost nearly all their slaves, others half. The Khojah and Banyan Indians posed no problem for they kept a register of births and deaths but all that Christie could say about the Arabs was that among the wealthier classes mortality was not very great while among the poorer classes it was 'most severe'. He had difficulty also in estimating mortality in the plantations, some of which were in parts of the island that he had never visited. However, his contacts with Captain Fraser's Mkokotoni sugar estate gave him a clue. Mortality there was estimated at 6.5 per cent, but the estate was exceptional in that it had a hospital for up to thirty patients, had obtained medical supplies in advance of the epidemic, and had imposed hygienic measures. The death rate in the neighbouring Arab estates, where no preventive measures were taken, and where the slaves were not as well fed as Fraser's workers, could therefore be assumed to be considerably higher.[2] After calculations along these lines, and presumably much scratching of his head, Christie concluded that mortality among Indians was 6.5 per cent, among Arabs at least 10%, and among Africans 25 per cent at the very lowest. The floating population, mainly the northern Arabs who swooped on Zanzibar every year to kidnap slaves, was also about 25% in his reckoning. He concluded that there must have been between 12,000 and 15,000 deaths in city and suburbs and 25,000 to 30,000 in the entire island – up to about 10% of the population. (Kirk's estimate of the total mortality was 10,000 but it seems unlikely that he went to the same lengths as Christie to gather information.)[3]

Other questions were trickier. Why had two communities – the Hindu Indians and the European residents – remained untouched by the epidemics? And why had the outbreak, after a sporadic beginning, suddenly flared up with multiple deaths in a single house in Melinde which then became the focus of a raging epidemic? The answer to the second question was to provide the clue to the first. Some time after the epidemic he had occasion to be in the house, and took the opportunity to examine it from top to bottom. On the first floor he found openings to two shafts, one leading to the cesspool and the other to the well, and on the ground floor the well shaft was open to the street, so that the public could help themselves to this highly prized water. The well and the cesspool were so situated that the contents of the latter were bound to pass into the former, and Christie also noted that servants would be as likely to empty slops into the one as into the other.

Until then Christie had been prepared to entertain the idea that cholera spread by aerial transmission – which was still the view of a minority of British doctors and the majority of British Indian ones. But now the logic of events was clear:

> The well received the soakage of the cesspool; it was
> extremely liable to direct contamination; the water was

largely used in the district; the deaths in the house preceded the general outbreak, and there was an absence of an otherwise adequate cause to account for the great mortality which prevailed within a short space of time among the population supplied from the well.

He was now becoming completely convinced that cholera was a waterborne disease in which infection was spread mainly by faecal contamination.[4]

But this fact alone could not account for Zanzibar's puzzling mortality pattern. It could not explain why the Hindu Indians and the European residents escaped the disease while the Muslim Indians and Europeans living on ships in the harbour were badly hit. Christie realised that location could not be the explanation. Arab houses, ravaged by the disease, were as favourably sited as those of their European neighbours, and there was nothing to choose between the houses of Muslim Indians and those of the Hindus. The European houses were more exposed than others to the sewage and impurities on the beach whereas Europeans on ships could breathe in the pure air around the north harbour. And African huts were scattered throughout the town.

Christie realised that manners and customs must provide the key. Though there was no physical segregation between the different sections of the community, he remarked that culturally and socially the divisions were almost as complete as walls of stone and lime. He was already an expert on this subject. From the time of his arrival in Zanzibar he had studied ethnic customs very closely. He had been inside the houses of his patients and was familiar with their way of life and living conditions, the layout of their dwellings, the details of their habits of hygiene. He had seen Arab bathrooms with large shafts to convey excrement to a dry well below. He had seen slave huts with no conveniences at all, where the evacuations of the sick were left to dry on the floor. He had noted the varying practices of the numerous African tribes on the island, could distinguish between the customs of different Indian sects and castes, was well versed in the theological differences between Arab Sunnis and Indian Shias, knew how the ways of the Omani Arabs differed from those of the Hadraumats, and how the lifestyle of the richer Arabs differed from that of the poorer.

And he knew where and how the different communities obtained their water supplies. Africans and many Arabs drank mainly from the town wells, which were open at the top and never cleaned out. Sometimes instead they would collect milky-looking water from country wells, which was highly prized for its sweet taste but just as polluted and faecal-smelling as the water from the town wells. The Khojahs, the biggest sect of Muslim Indians, also favoured this water. During the dry season, when there was no more than a trickle of liquid at the bottom of the wells, as many as 30 or 40 women used to squat round the top of the pit with their water jars, chatting while they waited for the water to percolate through. Sometimes they used the border of the well as a convenience while awaiting their turn to ladle the water into their jars by means of a coconut shell fastened to a long stick.

The Khojahs, as careless about the laws of health as they were about their water supplies, were the sickliest section of Zanzibar society, though they included many very wealthy men. Christie thought they would have died out quickly but for the fresh infusions from the west of India. The Hindus, or Banyans, though originating in the same part of India, had a very different attitude. They had strict caste rules about water – as Christie had learned when a Banyan ran off shrieking rather than have his ears syringed. Their water had to be drawn from their own wells and by one of their own caste or they would consider themselves defiled – even if the water had merely touched their clothing.[5] Christie was not even allowed to see Banyans drink water. When he was performing an operation which might result in fainting, the patient drank water behind a large scarf held up as a screen.

These strict caste rules saved the Hindus from cholera, with only one exception, a pawnbroker and seller of stolen goods from the lower end of the Banyans' economic scale. Christie happened to be passing the door of his shop at the time of his illness and seeing a small crowd inside he entered in his usual inquisitive way, realising that something unusual must be happening. It was the filthiest den he had ever seen and was full of thieves who had the sick pawnbroker at their mercy. He died within a few hours.

While the Banyans were protected by their religious rules, European residents were saved by their rules of hygiene. They would pay an African gang to fetch water from the healthiest of the country wells and then would conscientiously boil and filter it – a wise precaution since often it had been supplemented with water from the town wells. Unlike the Arabs, they couldn't tell its provenance by its taste.

Westerners living on ships had no chance to be pernickety. They fetched their water from two streams flowing onto the shore near the harbour. Africans in their thousands used to wade through and bathe in the same waters daily, and dirty clothing was washed there. When he was visiting merchant ships in harbour Christie would take the opportunity to examine the water tanks and thought that 'a more filthy decoction of every abomination could not be seen anywhere.' Once he saw excrement floating in a tank. A supply of drinking water was often taken on board just before sailing and not surprisingly cholera would break out after a few days at sea.[6] After the epidemic, rainwater from cement tanks in the town began to be used instead.

Christie noted that Europeans and Americans living on board ships survived for longer than other cholera victims, and 'endured a more dreadful struggle with death'. He had witnessed the appalling sufferings of a powerful young sailor who writhed in an agony of cramps, his muscles feeling like bars of iron or knotted iron ropes, his eyes appearing 'as if they would start from his sockets'. Africans, in contrast, were the quickest to die, often dropping dead in the street without previous symptoms. Arabs and Indians tended to survive for longer, even if only for a few hours, but westerners lived with the disease for several days.[7]

The only writing that Christie had done since arriving in Zanzibar consisted of his long letters to his brother, and it doesn't seem to have occurred to him that his cholera observations demanded a larger audience. However, one day just after the close of the epidemic Bishop Tozer passed on a letter from the secretary of the London Epidemiological Society requesting a report on the epidemic and its origins.

It was hardly the best time to do this: Christie was much in demand by his patients. The epidemic had left the survivors in a poor state of health. Almost immediately an epidemic of dengue fever broke out. This highly virulent disease was sometimes known as breakbone fever because the first symptoms were muscular pain and stiffness. Though sometimes fatal it resulted in no deaths during this outbreak, but spread extensively and attacked all ethnic groups. Three of Christie's European patients caught the disease, each one of them experiencing the first symptoms when arising from the dinner table. Christie was baffled. He was at a loss to know how to diagnose the disease and adopted the name of Ki-Dinga Pepo, which was given to it by some of Zanzibar's oldest inhabitants who remembered a similar outbreak nearly half a century before. Unaware that it was spread by mosquitoes he wrote in his notes that it somehow seemed to arise from the embers of the cholera epidemic.[8]

The report for the Epidemiological Society had to be pushed aside while Christie grappled with these problems, but once he got down to the task he tackled it with enthusiasm. Some investigative work was clearly called for since he had been asked to describe the origins of the epidemic as well as its course in Zanzibar. All that was known was that it had advanced from the north-west along the Masai caravan route to the east coast at Pangani. Christie determined to trace its course back to its origin and on from Zanzibar to its termination – and to do so without making any assumptions about how it was transmitted.

He had certain advantages. He had learned Swahili and as a doctor he met Africans from all parts of the interior. He had good background knowledge. His interest in ethnic customs extended far beyond Zanzibar, and he had developed a particular fascination with the great unknown and mysterious territory that was Masai country. He knew about the slave route through that territory, thanks to an investigation into Zanzibar's slave trade that he and Bishop Tozer had begun. He had access to the British consulate's records and had no inhibitions about button-holing traders and merchants who had been to the mainland, but he attached particular value to the accounts of Africans, believing that their veracity tended to be underestimated by Europeans.

In just a few weeks he pieced together an account of the origins not only of the recent epidemic but also East Africa's three earlier ones. After quizzing Arabs who were old enough to remember the epidemic of 1835-36, he was able to establish that it was first heard of in the Somali ports and that during the north-east monsoon it travelled southwards, following the course taken by the trading dhows until it reached Zanzibar. The second epidemic, in 1859-60, followed the same course and again coincided with the north-east monsoon, which was always accompanied by rapid communications from north to south, but not from south to north. The third epidemic, in 1865, broke out from the Somali ports only as the north-east monsoon was nearing its end. Fortunately for Zanzibar the south-west monsoon set in early that year, blocking the southward traffic before the epidemic reached the island. The fourth epidemic – actually a branch of the third, but Christie didn't know this at the time – was the one that had just ended, and unlike the others it travelled overland, reaching the coast via Masai country and later returning to the interior along a parallel line.

Christie heard tales of valuable loads of ivory being discarded when caravans from the interior reached the infected areas and survivors fled to their homes. At that stage he could only speculate that the pestilence had reached Masai territory through central Africa from the north, or across the country from the west. But he was able to state one thing with certainty:

'In all the turnings and windings of the cholera epidemic, there seems to have been one unvarying principle directing its course. It has invariably accompanied trade wherever its direction may have been.'

His report included a vivid account of the recent epidemic, with a particularly heart-rending account of the fate of the slaves who were transported to Zanzibar at that time. He analysed the differences between that epidemic and earlier ones, noting, for example, that very few Indians had died during the second epidemic. Before despatching his report he updated it by noting that the epidemic, although ended in Zanzibar, was still affecting the mainland. Six porters of a caravan which had just arrived at the coast had died of the disease, bringing it back to within 25 miles of the island.[9]

He then entrusted the report to the next ship bound for a British port, and expected to hear no more about it. It seemed unbelievable to him that anyone at home could have any interest in Zanzibar's epidemic. More than six months later, however, a naval doctor on a visiting ship handed him a back number of *The Lancet* for January, 1871.[10] It contained his report in the form of two articles, accompanied by an editorial describing them as 'opening an entirely new chapter of the history of epidemic cholera' and expressing 'our sense of the great value of Dr Christie's contribution'. The editorial noted that 'not a few of those who were presumed to have special knowledge of the subject' had been under the impression that the recent outbreak had been the first in East Africa. Even the delegates at the International Sanitary Conference at Constantinople had evidently been unaware of any cholera outbreaks in East Africa. The Epidemiological Society, however, had had its suspicions as the result of 'certain incidents' connected with the capture of slave boats in the Gulf of Aden, and when the opportunity arose to contact Bishop Tozer, the society had seized it.

The Lancet also reported that the Epidemiological Society had, with some difficulty, obtained extracts from Kirk's correspondence relating to cholera. These had been read at a meeting of the society but 'did not contribute any additional information of importance to that given in greater detail by Dr Christie'. The society was planning to discuss Christie's report at a meeting the following month.

That was not the end of the matter as far as Christie was concerned. The Epidemiological Society had asked him for more information but can hardly have been expecting the massive amount that he would accumulate. For the remaining three years of his stay in Zanzibar, and indeed for a while afterwards, he pursued his investigations. He interrogated caravan leaders, traders, missionaries who had worked in the interior, foreign travellers, Africans from mainland tribes. Sometimes he asked people to draw maps. He gave lists of questions to those about to set off for the mainland. He read widely in the writings of the explorers. He studied the trade routes, the geography and ethnology of the territory through which they passed.

This was a long-term project. A constant look-out had to be kept for intelligence from the mainland. Like cholera itself, the investigation was influenced by the seasons. 'Where there was a missing link in the track of the epidemic,' he later commented, 'it was necessary to wait patiently for another year, or until the season arrived when strangers from that part of the country visited the place.' This meant taking monsoons into account: 'The period of the north-east monsoon was the time for collecting information regarding the epidemic to the north of Zanzibar, and that of the south-west monsoon for news of the epidemic to the south.'[11]

He had one great advantage, apart from his deep interest in ethnic customs and particularly in the mysterious Masai country. The track of epidemics was less complicated than in countries with intricate networks of communication. Africans did not travel far beyond the boundaries of their own territories and the traders travelled along set routes in a predictable fashion. As Christie put it: 'The great highways of human intercourse are traversed only by traders at certain seasons of the year, and this uniformity of life is broken only by wars, and raids of marauders in quest of slaves and cattle.'[12]

A remarkable assortment of people found themselves drawn into the investigation. Captain Mohammed bin Hamees, for example, was able to fix the exact date of the arrival of cholera in Zanzibar in 1836, for he had been in London at the time and received a letter telling him that his grandfather had died in the epidemic.[13] Henry Spalding, an American trader living in Zanzibar, supplied the information that there had been an outbreak of cholera in Muscat two weeks before its arrival in Zanzibar in 1838. He had been told this by the man in charge of cargo on an American ship which had made an abrupt departure from the port, leaving half her cargo of dates behind.

When investigating the 1865 epidemic, the one that had stopped short of Zanzibar, Christie had the good luck to meet the German explorer Richard Brenner, a member of Baron von Decken's ill-fated expedition of the same year. After the baron had been brutally murdered, Brenner and others had managed to escape from hostile tribesmen – 'principally,' explained Christie, 'owing to Mr Brenner's unrivalled accuracy as a good shot'. Brenner told Christie that the members of expedition had witnessed cholera raging violently in the coastal towns – the Baron himself had had a severe attack – and when they reached the town of Barderah on the River Jubb in Somalia they learned that the area had earlier been affected by the disease. Brenner had made enquiries about its line of attack and learned that it had come from Gananah, further down the Jubb, on the trade route, and that it had reached there from Berbera on the Gulf of Aden, on the great caravan route down through Somalia. Berbera, with its annual fair, had already been noted by Christie as a likely dissemination point for cholera. He also learned from Brenner that the disease had susequently worked its way down river from Barderah to the Somali coast by the trade route, and from the coast would have undoubtedly have reached Zanzibar but for the early arrival of the south-west monsoon. Brenner drew a sketch map for Christie – who, presumably, was tactful enough not to repeat the disparaging view of Baron von Decken that he had earlier aired in one of his letters to Andrew.[14]

Brenner's evidence tied in with a piece of information that Christie had received from Netten Radcliffe, the honorary secretary of the London Epidemiological Society, who had learned that two cholera-infected slave dhows had been captured by a British naval ship in the Gulf of Aden in the spring of 1865, providing a vital link in the chronology of the epidemic. Here was added evidence that cholera spread by human agency. Christie reasoned that if the disease had been imported into Berbera at the opening of the annual fair by the first of the season's dhows from Bombay, this would have left just the right amount of time for it to travel along the trade route via Barderah to the coast and infect the two slave dhows heading into the Gulf of Aden in April and May, 1865.

Netten Radcliffe also provided vital information for his research into the origins of the 1869-70 epidemic.

All that Christie had been able to say about this epidemic in his report to the Epidemiological Society was that it had arrived in Zanzibar via Masai country. Radcliffe, however, pointed him in the right direction. He had investigated a particularly vicious outbreak among the 80,000 or more pilgrims assembled at Mecca for the jubilee pilgrimage of May 1865. After the jubilee ceremonies the pilgrims had immediately fled in all directions from the infected spot, one of the cholera tracks advancing into Abyssinia. Radcliffe conjectured that there was probably a connection between the Abyssinian outbreak and that of Zanzibar in 1869-70, but the problem was to find concrete evidence of this and to track the exact course.[15]

Very few of Zanzibar's Muslims went on pilgrimages to Mecca, so there were no clues to be found locally. However, Christie made ingenious use of two published accounts of a mission to Emperor Theodore of Abyssinia which had set out in 1865 to negotiate the release of British captives who were being held in the mountain fortress of Magdala. Making their way south from the Red Sea through war-torn country the three members of the expedition had more on their minds than epidemiology, but Christie was able to extract valuable evidence from their passing references to cholera – enough to establish that the disease had advanced southwards through Abyssinia, though its exact course could not be plotted because the country was in such a state of anarchy and confusion that travellers were often diverted from their regular routes.

Although warfare might sometimes speed the transmission of epidemic disease, Christie noted, it could have the opposite effect when 'the highways are occupied by thieves and murderers, as all bodies of troops are, in one point of view, whether regular or irregular.'

The situation was certainly confused. Hemmed in on all sides by rebels, Emperor Theodore was at the head of an army described by Christie as 'a disorderly rabble, with cholera clinging to its skirts'. The unfortunate members of the delegation were themselves captured and imprisoned in the Magdala fortress, where they were held until a British Indian relief expedition came to the rescue.[16] At that point the cholera trail went cold – Christie had to look elsewhere for clues.

He found some in the travel writings of Walter Plowden, British consul to Abyssinia, who described a journey from southern Abyssinia across the Blue Nile – impassable during the long rainy season – and into the land of the Galla tribes (now part of southern Ethiopia). After describing the great fair at Enarea, which sold the produce of the surrounding Galla countries, he gave useful information about the trade routes leading to and from it, and the pilgrim route from the Red Sea. Plowden had not travelled during the cholera epidemic but his account enabled Christie to see that the 1869 track of the disease must have passed through the country of the Galla peoples, and because of delays during the rainy season must have travelled at a slower pace than the 1865 epidemic, which took a more easterly and easier course.[17]

The thread of the investigation was then taken up by H.A. Heale, a Zanzibar resident who was asked by Christie to make inquiries during a trip to Brava, on the Somali coast to the east of Gallas country. Heale, who was murdered at Brava a few years later, reported that the cholera track had taken a sharp turn to run eastwards through Gallas country to the Somali coast, and the Somali chiefs at Brava agreed. Christie, however, rejected this advice. It did not fit with the timing of the rainy season or the tendency of the Gallas never to travel beyond their own boundaries. Every circumstance, he reckoned, confirmed the African reports that the epidemic had continued on a southwards track towards Masai country, where it had been raging when first heard of in Zanzibar.[18]

The final piece of the jigsaw was the track from Masai country to the coast opposite Zanzibar. The precise course was still unknown.

But now a Mombasa missionary, the Rev. Charles New, was in a position to find out more. Hearing that New had organised an expedition to explore Masai country with a view to establishing a mission station, Christie wrote to him and asked him to investigate the epidemic in that area. As the result of New's extensive inquiries Christie was able to track the exact cholera route and rate of travel from the country just west of Mount Kilimanjaro (which New climbed as far as the snowline) via Usambara country to the coast. He rated New's evidence highly both because of his linguistic skills and because he had no preconceived ideas about the distribution of cholera epidemics.[19]

Through prolonged investigations Christie amassed a huge amount of detail about the cholera trails. The accounts of New and others were woven together with references to cholera in the writings of the explorers, particularly Burton and Livingstone, and with Christie's own knowledge of tribal customs. He investigated anything that might have a bearing on the course of the epidemics, from Somali blood feuds to the horse market at Basso, where the animals were never groomed but were allowed to roll on the ground to keep them in condition for hard work. He discovered not only the main line of the cholera trails but in some cases their lateral extensions. His grasp of detail was remarkable.

If his argument seems circumstantial or speculative in places it has to be remembered that he went to huge lengths to establish the timetable of human travel and to compare it with the timing of the spread of the disease. He factored in the variables of weather conditions, terrain, and the great loops that had to be taken round hostile territory.

His main conclusions were that the cholera tracks to East Africa were identical with the trade routes – the seaboard route; the great caravan highway from Berbera on the Gulf of Aden down through the Ugahden province in Somalia to the River Jubb and thence to the coast; and the more westerly trade route through Abyssinia and the Galla lands of Somalia to Masai territory and east to Zanzibar. He was breaking new ground, not only proving Radcliffe's hypothesis correct by linking Mecca with the East African outbreaks but also demonstrating that the fair of Berbera was a major epidemic staging post – something that until then had been overlooked by epidemiologists. Above all he established conclusively that cholera travelled along human highways and that it travelled at human pace. It was beyond argument that the epidemics had been spread by human agency.

This discovery might not seem particularly startling some twenty years after John Snow had made the same point through his famous piece of detective work at London's Broad Street pump and subsequent treatise, which had indicated that cholera was a waterborne disease caused by faecal contamination. Yet Snow's findings had not been universally accepted.

The argument between contagionists and miasmatists – one of the great medical debates of the era – was to rage on till the close of the nineteenth century. Certainly by the 1870s the majority of British doctors had become converted to contagionism, and many of the remaining miasmatists had at least modified their beliefs to accommodate a degree of contagionism. Few now held to the original belief, prevalent earlier in the century, that cholera spread entirely from poisonous emissions emanating from rotting vegetation or human filth. But pockets of resistance still existed, not least in British India.

The Indian Medical Service – a branch of the British Indian Government – had a number of reasons for wishing to cling to this theory. Lord Mayo's administration had inherited an alarming budget deficit. The economic climate was unfavourable to the creation of new waterworks and other expensive measures that would be necessary if the contagionists were right and cholera was a waterborne disease. If the miasmatists were right it would be enough to tackle the accumulations of filth on the streets. In addition maritime quarantine, also associated with contagionism, would be bad for trade – an irony since it was the expansion of India's maritime trade that had exported the disease to most of the rest of the world. There was also nervousness, in those post-Mutiny years, about stirring popular unrest through heavy-handed preventive measures, particularly in the case of Hindu pilgrimages. And since India was the only country where cholera was endemic there was a reluctance among its medical profession to take advice from upstart epidemiologists elsewhere.[20]

All this had a bearing on Zanzibar, where the British consulate was still under the wing of the Bombay Government, its staff being appointed in India. Perhaps it was not surprising that the consulate had played such a low-key role on the approach of the cholera epidemic in 1869. Christie's findings demonstrated the inadequacy of this policy.

Along with Netten Ratcliffe's investigations into the cholera outbreaks at Mecca they pulled the rug from under the theories of the Indian Medical Service – or would do when Christie eventually decided that his work was worthy of being turned into a book. The IMS had also been investigating the 1869 epidemic. Dr James Bryden, an Edinburgh University graduate and the British Indian Government's chief adviser on cholera, reported that the 'seeds' of the disease had swarmed to East Africa 'like a plague of locusts', borne along by monsoon currents. Bryden, basing his deductions on statistical analysis, had apparently been influenced by the early work of the English epidemiologist William Farr, although unlike Farr he never became a convert to contagionism.[21] Christie, with his investigative nose and wide-ranging interests, was more similar to the great John Snow. In its own way his achievement was scarcely less remarkable. The great highways of Africa were his Broad Street.

CHAPTER 12

Sultan's Doctor – Consul's Enemy

WHEN CHRISTIE looked out of his waterfront house he could see signs of change in Zanzibar. Writing to his brother in mid-1870, not long after the close of the cholera epidemic, he noted that there were eight square-rigged vessels in the harbour, with a dozen more expected over the following month. Christie could now see that 'the central portions of Africa from South to North will eventually be occupied by Europeans.' The Suez Canal had opened in November, 1869, the month when the epidemic had arrived on the island. East Africa had been brought closer to Europe. Merchandise and mail could be exchanged much more easily.

With this boost to Zanzibar's trade, Sir William Mackinnon, who had earlier dropped his plans for a steamship service to Zanzibar, renewed his interest in the island. Regular shipping lines from Zanzibar to Aden and Mozambique were started, and a British India agency was opened on the island. Christie's friend Captain Fraser was placed in charge of it but, with his business floundering after the destruction of his sugar crop by a hurricane, he was fairly quickly replaced by a member of Mackinnon's Glasgow office.[1]

Another change would closely affect Christie. In October, 1870, Sultan Majid died. He had presided over a period of reasonable prosperity but was not highly regarded by his European contemporaries (although some present-day historians rate him more generously). With his lethargic temperament he seemed to fit in with

Christie's view of Arab rule as 'in spirit opposed to every idea of progress' and 'out and out conservative'. However when Majid was succeeded by his more energetic and strong-minded brother, Seyyid Bargash, Christie accepted a post as his physician. 'Although the emoluments are not large,' he reported to Andrew, 'the position is good and perhaps may lead to something.' In particular he hoped that Bargash would establish a hospital on the island.[2]

Meanwhile his practice was expanding and he began to think that it might become possible to appoint an assistant and go home 'for a year or so'. The work involved in running a single-handed practice was now 'dreadfully hard'. His researches into the origins of cholera epidemics made more demands on his time, as did his writing. He had been asked for a further contribution to *The Lancet,* had been made a corresponding member of the Epidemiological Society, was busy on articles for the *US Medical Journal* and the *Transactions of the Medical and Physical Society of Bombay,* and was writing reports for the *Times of India.* In the summer of 1871 he declared himself 'quite done up' from all the writing.

There was also domestic stress: Betsy Christie had developed chronic dysentry, though she was well enough to accompany her husband to a grand dinner for Admiral Cockburn, commander-in-chief of the East Indies station, who was spending several weeks in Zanzibar – an occasion which brought 'a grand turn-out of brilliant uniforms'.[3] Nevertheless his wife's condition worried Christie, and unfortunately occurred at a time when he had an extra workload because of the amount of sickness in the town. Just possibly there was another source of stress. The Christies were childless, and would remain so throughout their marriage, but there is documentary evidence that at some stage a child was born and died either at birth or in early infancy.

Not surprisingly, a testy note was evident in some of Christie's letters. In addition to orders for surgical instruments and medical items such as iodine of potassium and monthly supplies of vaccine, Christie made many demands of his brother – send a first-rate Dunlop cheese; send six merino vests, a gold brooch and earrings, a saddle girth, three pairs of shoes, a *Glasgow Herald*, a large album, a fish slice, two dresses, visiting cards, a lamp, whalebone stays for Betsy since steel ones would be unsuitable for the climate . . . also 'I am wearing my last pair of slippers.' The resulting consignments were not always graciously received. A bonnet sent out for Betsy 'will be all right, though perhaps very grotesque'; the Dunlop cheese was 'excellent but I thought it was too new and rich'; a batch of jelly 'was doubtless excellent but I am sorry to say the cans were empty.' Andrew also sent out an assortment of goods for his brother to sell – guns and lamps, which fetched a fair price, though this was offset by high freight charges.

Christie was less pleased by the 'quite unsaleable' scarves that arrived on spec from Kilmarnock. He warned Andrew in future to dispatch only goods that had been ordered. Despite his unfortunate experiences as an acting sugar factory manager some vestiges of entrepreneurial ambition remained. He promised to send Andrew samples of the fez-like caps commonly worn in Zanzibar, which were made in France or Switzerland. 'I do not see why they cannot be made at Stewarton,' he told his brother. Later he asked Andrew for estimates of the cost of building an iron bridge for the Sultan.[4]

The traffic between Kilmarnock and Zanzibar was two-way. In return for the consignments of clothing and medical supplies Andrew Christie and his wife were sent 'a box containing a few Zanzibar odds and ends' including shells, collections of entymology, mats, gazelle skins (which Christie suggested might be made into a pair of slippers), a few pieces of gum copal with small insects embedded in them, and a small bottle of attar of roses which the Sultan had given to Christie's wife. Later he sent hippopotamus teeth, whale teeth and the saw of a sawfish with one tooth missing. To his niece, Mary, he sent a gift of a grey parrot from central Africa – 'a nice affectionate creature and very tame' although Christie confessed it was a poor specimen in comparison with his own pet parrot, a 'reckless scoundrel' which had just eaten the table covers. Mary's parents may have been less than delighted to learn that it had to be let out of his cage from time to time despite having a habit of destroying books and papers. Despite being a poor specimen it survived the voyage, though nothing is known about its life in Scotland since Andrew's letters to Zanzibar have not been preserved along with his brother's.[5]

Soon James and Betsy Christie were faced with domestic havoc worse than anything their parrot could create. Zanzibar's inhabitants had thought that they were safely outside the cyclone belt but in mid-April, 1872 a squally south-westerly gale reached hurricane force and began to rotate. The streets became torrents, the spray flew over the houses, the flags above some of the consulates were ripped to shreds. African huts were swept away and inside the houses along the waterfront cascades of water ran down staircases and roofs were blown away – the Christies lost their verandah roof. The iron roofs over the Sultan's palace were lifted into the sea with a single blast and his ships were all lost, along with other craft in the harbour, including numerous dhows which were driven against the reefs. Several bodies were washed ashore. Outside the town, crops in the plantations were destroyed.

After a brief lull a second hurricane, this time from the north, blew in more doors and windows, causing some of the waterfront houses to be evacuated. The violent sea swept away the stone embankment and wooden piles protecting the foundations of the British, German and US consulates. With the tide rising and water beating against the large house of the Universities Mission, Bishop Tozer – with an invalid in his arms – and the other occupants sought refuge in the middle of the night at the nearby house of a German merchant, a little further from the waterfront. Bishop Tozer's sister, then on an extended stay in Zanzibar, thought the town with its roofless houses looked as if it had been bombarded. Christie remarked that if the hurricane had lasted for just two or three hours longer every house along the beach would have been swept away.[6]

He assessed his losses at more than £500, but soon had to add considerably to this total. Ten days after the cyclone a terrible gale brought torrents of rain 'such as I have never seen even in Zanzibar'.

Without the verandah roof the Christies' house was alarmingly exposed to the storm. The rain battered through the walls, which had become sponge-like, and flooded the house. As Christie later reported to his brother, 'we had simply to bale out the water from the rooms all day'. Towards evening he thought the whole house would come down and the soaked couple found refuge with a neighbour. He had never, Christie wrote to his brother, passed such a wretched day in his life and he didn't understand how his wife had survived it.

He feared for Zanzibar's future. The crops that slaves were allowed to grow for themselves had been destroyed and they had no means of buying any imported food. Christie thought that gangs of starving slaves might come into the town for plunder and was critical of the British consul for not requesting a gunboat to be stationed in the harbour as a means of escape if necessary.[7] His fears, which were shared by no one except his friend Captain Fraser, proved largely groundless, although Christie himself was robbed of some bottles of medicine – which were then offered for sale to him.

However the cyclone did have serious long-term consequences for the island. With two-thirds of the clove and coconut plantations destroyed, the economy was more than ever dependent on the slave trade – and this at a time when the British Government was stepping up its efforts to limit the trade as the prelude to negotiating its total abolition. It could not be abolished outright since Zanzibar was not a British colony, but a treaty with the Sultan in 1847 had restricted the ancient and lucrative trade to his African dominions, both on Zanzibar and the mainland. The ban on the export of slaves outside these territories was difficult to enforce, and the Royal Navy had very limited success in policing the trade.

The squadron charged with preventing the illegal export of slaves consisted usually of seven or eight small cruisers stationed at intervals along the African and Arabian coasts. Smaller boats, manned by twenty or thirty sailors, were launched to chase slave dhows through shallow waters. Trapped dhows would make a dash for the shore and slaves would be ordered to make for the land, many of them drowning in the attempt and others left stranded on a deserted stretch of coast without food or water. Captured slave dhows were often simply scuttled or burned on the spot instead of being taken to Zanzibar so that those responsible could be tried in the Vice-Admiralty court. Captured slaves were sent to Bombay or to the Seychelles or Mauritius to lead a life of forced labour on the plantations. Some of the children were placed in the charge of the Universities Mission in Zanzibar.[8]

Christie was horrified by these activities. He was in total accord with the Government's ultimate aim of negotiating an end to the trade, but utterly opposed to the use of the navy in what he saw as a crude attempt to enforce the treaty with the Sultan. From his house he had a grandstand view of boarding parties at work. 'I myself have seen dhows boarded in Zanzibar harbour, and they have been burned and sunk in the harbour, and this in direct opposition to the terms of the treaty,' he wrote to Andrew.[9]

His outrage at British tactics formed a recurrent theme in his letters. 'There is one subject on which I am fierce, nay even savage, and that is, the means adopted to suppress the slave trade,' he wrote not long after his arrival in Zanzibar. 'Legalised sea pirates, murderers, robbers, I call them. I know. I have seen it.' He was particularly angered by the sight of a British man-of-war whose captain was guilty of 'wholesale robbery'. Christie thought that if his attacks on the native shipping had continued for much longer 'the English residents would have had a good chance of getting their throats cuts.'

He personally knew a respectable Indian merchant who had despatched a dhow to the neighbouring island of Pemba with a cargo of wood and a large sum of money for the purchase of coconuts. A little later he heard that the boat had been seized, the money stolen, the dhow and cargo burned, and the crew taken to the Seychelles. It angered him that such people had no redress whatever but had to submit in silence. It angered him too that when a few slaves were seized the officers and crew of the ship responsible for their capture were paid far more money than would be needed to buy the slaves and free them. The attempted suppression of the slave trade was in his view 'one of the greatest farces of the age' in that it was of no practical value and entailed more suffering and degradation on the African race than if no attempt in that way were made'.[10]

Christie's denunciations of the abuses by the naval patrol sometimes seem more passionate than his hatred of slavery itself. Yet he was scarcely exaggerating. The looting of Arab dhows, whether they were actually slave-running or not, is well documented and Christie was not alone in his opposition. The US consul in Zanzibar, Francis Webb, estimated that 70 Arab trading vessels had been burned in a single year, including many non-slavers. The Americans on the island feared that such ravages would have a ruinous effect on trade. Many Americans in Zanzibar had fought for the north in the Civil War and were in sympathy with British anti-slavery sentiment but, like Christie, they thought that more sensitive tactics should be adopted. The American position was particularly delicate at a time when their trade with Zanzibar was picking up again after the dangers to their shipments posed by Confederate vessels during the American Civil War.[11]

For a while such criticisms seemed to have an effect. In 1869 a Foreign Office official reported that the naval patrol's operation could not be justified and that it 'would not be tolerated for a month by any European power if their vessels were seized and condemned without a hearing.' The Foreign Office warned Kirk not to exceed his remit in dealing with slave trade cases. Orders were given that in future trials should be held in the Vice-Admiralty Court in Zanzibar and the naval squadron was instructed not to destroy captured dhows unless in exceptional circumstances. Many slave dhows were formally condemned in the court but navigational difficulties and limited fuel supplies meant that others continued to be dealt with in a summary way.[12]

The naval patrol was not only a blunt weapon but ineffectual, because of the difficulties of distinguishing between illegal slave dhows and those that were permitted under the 1847 treaty. There were signs that the slave trade was actually on the increase. This was happening at a time when, with the Atlantic slave trade successfully halted, British philanthropic sentiment was turning increasingly to the human traffic described by Livingstone in East Africa. Against that background a Commission on the East African Slave Trade was appointed by the Foreign Office in 1870 and a year later reported that 'the time had come when the Sultan should be pressed gradually to diminish the legal export of slaves . . . with a view to its ultimate abolition'.

Although burdened by writing commitments Christie set about preparing a counterblast to the Commission's report. He believed that the way to end the slave trade was by paying compensation to the Sultan for his loss of revenue and by establishing alternative trades – the influence of Livingstone, who believed in the civilising mission of trade, was perhaps evident here.

Christie's paper [13] gave a detailed and authoritative account of slavery in Zanzibar, likening the great Arab landowners to feudal overlords and emphasising their patriarchal role, and the loyalty of their slaves towards them. He explained that slaves were allowed to spend some of their time working for themselves. 'There are many slaves in Zanzibar who are persons of considerable wealth and importance and the owners of other slaves,' he insisted. The Arab slave system, he argued, was more benign than the Anglo-Saxon equivalent, which had been 'characterised by circumstances of extreme atrocity, the slave being regarded simply as an animal'. He suggested that this was because Christians held slaves in defiance of their own religious tenets whereas Muslims did so in accordance with their religious beliefs. Aware, no doubt, that his words might well be read as a defence of Arab-style slavery, he added: 'This does not mitigate the *essential* evil of slavery, nor does it form any reason against the suppression of slavery; it merely indicates certain difficulties in its accomplishment.'

He was scathing about the Commission's failure to recognise these difficulties and mocked its statement that because of the demand for free labour in Zanzibar liberated slaves would not cost the Government anything for their maintenance. 'A greater amount of absurdity could not be compressed into less space,' he commented, citing the example of 700 freed slaves of whom no fewer than 143 were on his hospital list, all of them severe cases. He went as far as to say that: 'During the whole of my experience as a medical man, as house surgeon in a large general hospital and in visiting hospitals in Great Britain and the Continent, I have never seen such revolting cases of disease.'

No worthwhile scheme could be without expense to the Government, he argued, and proceeded to give his own solution: slavery would die a natural death if the interior could be opened up by roads and natural resources developed. The Africans of the interior would then have goods to exchange for the articles brought by the traders and would have no need to capture neighbouring tribesmen to sell as slaves. Sultan Bargash, he added, had just such a scheme for constructing a road as far as Khutu on the great ivory caravan route, but he would have difficulty in funding the project. The money spent annually by the British Government on the suppression of the slave trade would, he added pointedly, go far to cover the cost. Christie also suggested that one or more of the small islands fringing the coast would be 'a suitable starting-point for an East African Liberia for freed slaves. Then their liberty would be a boon, not a mere name, a caricature on liberty,' he concluded.

He sent his paper to a London bookseller who published it in pamphlet form, with contributions from Bishop Tozer and Captain Fraser. Tozer concentrated on the lack of care provided for liberated slaves and criticised the Commission for ignoring the subject. Fraser, a hardline opponent of any plan to end the slave trade, claimed that if the maritime slave trade were to be abolished, wealthy Arabs would move to the mainland and start a slave market there.

By the time the pamphlet was published a Commons Select Committee was set up to inquire into the slave trade and provide the Foreign Office with a more democratic mandate than the Commission could provide. Copies of the pamphlet were sent to everyone who gave evidence and to all members of the Opposition as well as to the British

Consulate in Zanzibar. Christie awaited the response. He was in fighting mood. 'I am itching to have an attack made so that I may have an opportunity of fighting the so-called anti-slavery party,' he wrote to his brother. 'In honest sincerity I say that the means adopted and carried out for the suppression of the slave trade . . . is a scandal to any civilised country.'[14]

The pamphlet had, of course, no effect on policy. The Select Committee recommended not only that the naval squadron be strengthened but that pressure should be put on the Sultan to sign a new treaty abolishing rather than merely restricting the slave trade. Gladstone's Government adopted the recommendations. A special mission headed by Sir Bartle Frere, the highly regarded former Governor of Bombay, was sent to Zanzibar to implement them. The members of the mission arrived in the Admiralty yacht HMS *Enchantress* in January, 1873, and dropped anchor at the British consulate, where John Kirk was waiting to go on board to welcome them.

Next day Frere and his men walked from the consulate to the Sultan's palace on the waterfront, its blood-red flag flying aloft. The narrow streets were thronged with Arab and African onlookers. Several dozen uniformed British and Americans added to the spendour of the scene and the Sultan's guard of Arab and Persian soldiers lined the street. The Sultan stepped forward some 30 yards from his door to greet them – never before, reported Frere later, had he been known to advance so far to welcome any visitor. A letter from Queen Victoria was handed over and received with signs of veneration, and the following day the Sultan was welcomed at the *Enchantress* with a 21-gun salute. The mission had got off to a splendid start but the negotiatons had yet to begin.[15]

Christie was soon given an opportunity to press his case. Frere invited him to call on him aboard the *Enchantress*. It was a long interview but the slave trade was not the only subject. There was a surprise for Christie: Frere asked him to become British consul at Ujiji, the Arab trading settlement on Lake Tanganyika where Stanley had met Livingstone. The set-up was strange – he would be 'under the Sultan's sanction but with consular powers'. Cynics might have suspected that this was a ploy by Kirk to get Christie out of Zanzibar, but Christie was ready for a change from what he described as his 'artificial life', and he had always felt drawn to the interior. By the time he dined with Frere a day or two later he had decided to accept.[16]

The appointment, of course, depended on the Sultan as well as the Foreign Office, but since Christie was after all the Sultan's doctor, there could surely be no problem – particularly in the cordial atmosphere in which the Frere mission had begun its work.

Soon the atmosphere became less friendly. Bargash conferred with his family and with his council of about fifty sheiks. The Frere mission received word that the draft treaty presented earlier to the Sultan had been peremptorily rejected. The sheiks were not the only people creating obstacles. Before Frere's arrival in Zanzibar the Foreign Office had been successfully canvassing the support of the governments of the US, France and Germany. But their representatives in Zanzibar had minds of their own. The acting US consul, John F. Webb (no relation to the consul, Francis Webb, who had been driven home by illness), feared that British policy would destabilise trade and he also suspected that Britain had strategic motives. Frere's mission, he believed, was part of a scheme to drive out business competitors. In addition he and the other consuls shared Christie's dislike of John Kirk, whose high-handed attitude was revealed in a missive to the Foreign Office in 1870 in which he said that 'all the other consuls were upset at his success with the Sultan who now treated the consulate with proper respect and as taking precedence in everything without question'.

When the US government gave Webb a letter in support of British policy to hand to the Sultan he saw to it that it was neutered in translation into Arabic.[17] The French consul, Charles de Vienne, also refused to back the British despite the promises of his government (though Frere had felt that these promises were less than wholehearted). The French Government explained that de Vienne 'had got entangled in the cause of interests hostile to the policy he is now instructed to obey'. Theodore Schultz, the German consul, was also cold towards the Frere mission, at least until his orders arrived from Berlin.[18]

The consuls were not the only ones intent on making life difficult for Frere. The Sultan called in Captain Fraser for a 'long discussion' and while there is no record of what was said, it may certainly be assumed that his advice was not helpful to the mission.[19]

Christie's own view was that the Sultan should be offered compensation for ending the slave trade, and that Europe and the US should contribute to the expense in an attempt to wipe out not only the slave trade but slavery itself – ending the trade would be no use as long as slavery existed. He must have pressed this view upon Frere at their meetings. But the idea was not acted upon by Frere because an offer of compensation was reckoned to be insulting. There were ways round this, such as writing off debts, but rather than make proposals Frere left it to the Sultan to make suggestions.[20] The Sultan was silent. The negotiations collapsed.

Frere sailed for home after leaving instructions with Kirk, who had finally been promoted to consul after his long spell of doing the work in an acting capacity. Kirk was instructed to abrogate the Sultan's treaty rights to ship slaves within his own dominions and to close all slave markets immediately, but the Crown law officers ruled against this unilateral abrogation of the 1845 treaty. The Foreign Secretary, Lord Granville, sent a masterly diplomatic communique to Kirk: 'If you have proceeded to carry out Sir Bartle Frere's instructions you should, with as little ostensible retraction as possible, withhold further measures in that direction.' [21]

Instead, the Sultan was to be told that he was required to sign the new treaty or face a British naval blockade. After further persuasion by Kirk, backed up by Francis Webb, who took a more realistic view than his namesake when he resumed the position of US consul, the Sultan signed. On the same day he ordered the closure of Zanzibar slave market. Six months later, on Christmas Day, 1873, the foundation stone for a new Anglican cathedral was laid on the site of the former slave market.

Several years later John Kirk was given a knighthood. The Sultan was granted his request of a trip to England, where he caught the public imagination and helped to put Zanzibar on the map. And Christie seems to have heard no more about the Ujiji post.

CHAPTER 13
Search

C HRISTIE had said goodbye to David Livingstone in March, 1866, but had not put him out of his mind. His letters to Kilmarnock made frequent references to news of the explorer – or, more often, to the lack of news. Occasionally Livingstone sent letters to the British consulate, but it annoyed Christie that the news was never released in Zanzibar until after it had been dispatched to Britain. Still, there were unofficial sources, such as the reports of caravan leaders and porters returning from the interior, though some of their accounts were more reliable than others. Christie also had his own contacts and made his own inquiries. When, for example, there were widespread rumours of Livingstone's death in 1868 Christie was, he said, 'much abused here for being the means of throwing doubt on the fact of Livingstone's death'. He claimed to have been 'the first to ascertain here that he was actually alive and in the neighbourhood of Ujiji, but the intelligence was sent home without any acknowledgement'.[1] Letters were received from Livingstone at the British Consulate in late 1869, but from then on there was silence.

When H.M. Stanley arrived in Zanzibar in January 1871, he told no one except the US consul, Francis Webb, that he meant to find Livingstone – although John Kirk easily saw through the deception after Stanley had pumped him with questions about the explorer.[2] Christie, who was not privy to Stanley's plan despite his friendship with Webb, merely wrote to his brother that 'Mr Stanley does not indicate his proposed line of travel as that will depend on circumstances.' Like everyone else in Zanzibar he was impressed at the speed and efficiency with which this totally inexperienced explorer prepared his expedition. Christie thought it indicated 'a resolution and perseverence capable of successfully encountering more than ordinary difficulties'. He thought that, barring accidents, the American would show 'that African travel is not such a difficult and dangerous affair as has been represented'.[3]

But soon he was dealing with the first casualty of the expedition. While Stanley and his men were still encamped at Bagamoyo on the mainland coast the chief butler, who had quickly realised that Stanley was likely to prove a hard master, was given permission to visit friends in Zanzibar for a few days. While there he deliberately shot one of his eyes out, and received a note from Christie confirming the extent of the injury.[4]

Christie maintained contact with Stanley during his epic journey. In August, 1871 Stanley wrote to him from Myanyembe country with a request for various items of medicine, including sulphate of quinine, alum, iodine of potassium, tincture of henbane, and sulphate of zinc, as well as a catheter. Stanley directed that the medicines should be packed in cotton in a small, light box, the whole thing to weigh no more than 5 lbs. He also asked Christie for 'a few instructions concerning the uses of the above medicines, and any other advice which your medical experience would suggest.' As an interim payment Stanley sent six gold coins with the soldiers charged with delivering the letter. He wrote that he would be back in Zanzibar in six months (eight, in the event) and would repay any loan with interest, and would also thank Christie heartily 'for the aid you furnished this traveller when in distress'. After meeting Livingstone he wrote again to Christie, declining an offer of another delivery of medicine from Zanzibar and adding that he had already left the explorer 'more medicines than even he will require for 10 years to come'.[5]

Christie, meanwhile, had never stopped believing that Livingstone was still alive. 'I believe that he does not write because he has no great desire to do so,' he remarked in a letter to Andrew. Before hearing that Livingstone had been found, and evidently still unaware of the real purpose of Stanley's expedition, he and Captain Fraser had decided to organise a search party. They spent $500 of their own money organising the expedition but the man in charge defected to someone else who was offering more money for some different purpose.[6]

When Stanley returned to the island in mid-1872, with his account of his meeting with Livingstone, he seems to have expected that Christie and Fraser would be annoyed at having been misled by him. Instead, he was touched by the warmth of their praises.

'Instead of feeling annoyed that I had done what they had intended to do, they were among my most enthusiastic admirers,' he wrote in his book *How I found Livingstone*, published later that year.[7]

Among the bonds between Stanley and Christie was a strong dislike of John Kirk. During Stanley's first conversation with the consul he had noted that Kirk's face became animated only when he was relating some of his hunting feats. Later he spent a dreary evening at one of the Kirks' regular Tuesday soirees – 'the pleasure of these evenings the civilised community of Zanzibar ignore,' he commented.[8] On his return to Zanzibar after his meeting with Livingstone he had more serious grievances against the consul. At Bagamoyo he had seen supplies intended for Livingstone mouldering in a hut three months after having been dispatched from Zanzibar because the escorts engaged by Kirk had not troubled to take them any further. Stanley was annoyed that Kirk had evidently not crossed to Bagamoyo to see them on their way. Kirk accused Stanley of having turned Livingstone against him, but in fact Livingstone had sent Kirk two letters of complaint about the mishandling of supplies several weeks before his meeting with Stanley.[9] (An investigation was later held by Sir Bartle Frere, who exonerated Kirk.)

The feud escalated when the mischievous Fraser wrote to the *Bombay Gazette* to say that Livingstone had brought grave charges against Kirk and to repeat the story about the delayed supplies at

Bagamoyo. A summary of the letter was cabled to London and appeared in the *Standard*. Kirk's allies rushed into print in his defence, fearing that permanent damage had been done to his career.[10] The controversy gathered steam when Stanley went on a lecture tour of Britain, denouncing Kirk at every turn – even in Edinburgh, where Kirk had gained his medical degree. He was critically received in some quarters but warmly welcomed in Scotland where he was seen as the rescuer of the national hero. Cheering crowds greeted him at railway stations and public meetings and he was feted at civic banquets. Christie's brother Andrew went to hear him lecture in Glasgow in October, 1872, but Christie was annoyed that his brother had not taken the opportunity to call on Stanley. 'He was under many obligations to me, and I'm sure he would have been glad to have seen you,' he commented.[11]

Before leaving Zanzibar for his lecture tour Stanley had recruited an expedition of 57 carriers to go to Livingstone's assistance. On the night before his departure he told Christie that Kirk had refused to take any charge of forwarding fresh supplies. Since Stanley was anxious about the supplies Christie agreed to cross to the mainland the next day and convey the caravan across the river Pangani, 'in case of difficulties preventing the natives from doing so'. The coastal country was flooded, and the party, reported Christie, 'were in mud or water nearly to their shoulders'.[12] In August, 1872 the party made contact with Livingstone, who sang their praises. When he died nine months later most of them were still with him and helped to bear his body back to the coast.

The standard accounts state that Livingstone's devoted African followers, Joseph Wainwright, Chumo and Susi eviscerated his body in order to transport it back to Zanzibar. Christie, however, gave a rather different version to the *Natal Colonist* a year later. His former cook, Frajella, whose freedom he had purchased, was according to Christie the one who had prepared the body. As well as assisting Christie during operations he had seen his master dissect bodies and volunteered to perform this necessary service before the long journey back.[13]

When the party reached the coast in mid-February, 1874, they were conveyed to Zanzibar by HMS *Valiant*. Christie, said to have been the last person to have seen Livingstone before he left Zanzibar, now had the task of identifying his remains. The body was taken to the British consulate where, in the absence of John Kirk, who was on home leave, it was examined by Christie and John Robb, British consular surgeon. Robb had never met Livingstone but Christie was able to testify: 'I knew Dr Livingstone formerly and from the peculiar formation of the skull I concluded that the body was that of Dr Livingstone.' Later, in London, the identification was confirmed on the basis of a severe injury that Livingstone had sustained in his arm and shoulder as the result of a mauling by a lion during his very first African journey. [14]

* * *

Identifying Livingstone's remains was one of the last things that Christie did in Zanzibar. There was little to keep him there now. His restlessness had been evident at the time of Sir Bartle Frere's mission when there had seemed a possibility of a diplomatic posting in Ujiji. When this fell through he spoke of getting an exchange with a ship's doctor and going to Natal for a month, but no more was heard of this plan. With Kirk confirmed as British consul, and growing more powerful all the time, Zanzibar had become a less congenial place.

His friend Bishop Tozer had gone back to England. He had never recovered from the effects of the hurricane. One of his arms had become partly paralysed and in order to write he had to twist his hand into a claw-like position. 'He is utterly shattered, knocked down and out of heart,' wrote his sister to a friend. 'His head is so bad he can't bear the boys' voices, and gets irritable even at the cry of a cat, drags himself in and out of the chapel and meals . . . .' He also had 'a troublesome throat' – 'but no wonder,' wrote his sister, 'with all his shouting in chapel, everlasting talking and singing and reading'. Eventually he was persuaded to take a holiday in the Seychelles, and he never returned to Zanzibar. He resigned from his post in April 1873, and later lived a life of self-imposed poverty in Devon, having apparently given away all his possessions except his bible and his toothbrush.[15]

Although Christie was the Universities Mission's doctor his letters gave no hint of any deep interest in its activities, impressive though these were. Both a boys' school and mission college and a girls' school had been established, with the older children – mainly liberated slaves – acting as pupil-teachers. A printing press had been set up, producing elementary textbooks in Swahili. Services were held in both Swahili and English and a mission station had been established on the mainland, a day's journey from the coast. Although Christie never mentioned the Mission's activities in his letters, or indeed gave any indication of interest in religion generally, Bishop Tozer had nevertheless been his ally in the campaign against the tactics used by the navy to suppress the slave trade, and their ideas were in tune. Just as Christie was annoyed at the consulate for imposing its own system of justice over local customs, so Tozer believed that 'there is a danger . . . in trying to make our converts black Englishmen.' He was annoyed when a shoemaker was sent out to join the mission because this seemed like depriving people of a second pair of hands – his boys, he said, could pick up a needle with their feet and place it in someone's hands. 'It is wonderful,' he commented, 'how much wisdom after a time you will discover in the use of customs which at first sight seem barbarous.'[16]

Christie's friend Captain Fraser, meanwhile, was still on the island but in deep trouble. His business had been going from bad to worse, and so it seems had his behaviour. Early in 1872 he attempted to break up a street brawl between his servants and those of an Arab neighbour, and became drawn into the stramash himself. Summoned along with his neighbour to the British consulate he hurled abuse both at the Arab and at John Kirk. When Kirk and the Arab finally left the room to speak privately, Fraser followed and according to Kirk 'continued his harangue'. Later, and presumably soberer, Fraser said he would not blame Kirk if he expelled him from Zanzibar, though he also said that what he liked was a good stand-up fight.[17]

Soon after this incident he had more serious problems on his hands when the hurricane flattened the sugar plantation, adding to the troubles brought about by bad management. When Fraser went on leave to Scotland later that year, some people thought that he would never return. 'He is nearly ruined, and his sugar plantation and great establishment at Mkokotoni destroyed, so I suppose he succumbs poor man, and won't return,' wrote Bishop Tozer's sister, as prolific a letter-writer as Christie.[18]

It had been arranged that during his stay in Scotland Fraser would visit Andrew Christie in Kilmarnock. 'Show Captain Fraser all the hospitality you can, without putting yourself much about,' Christie instructed his brother. 'You can always give him a good whisky and water and a drive out if he wishes to see any of the South Ayrshire farms.'[19] In the event Fraser didn't turn up in Kilmarnock – but, contrary to the predictions of some and no doubt the hopes of others, he did return to Zanzibar for a brief struggle with his failing business before finally escaping, late in 1874, to Natal with his cargo of sugar.

But Christie himself had left the island by that time. In addition to his restlessness, his health was probably a consideration. Some of his bouts of fever were perhaps worse than he indicated in his letters. During one bout in 1872 he was described as being 'extremely ill in fever' and 'delirious'. Because he was incapacitated a ship's doctor had to be called in to attend a leading member of the Universities Mission, Lewin Pennell, who was also suffering from fever and who died a few days later.[20]

Christie's forty-fifth birthday was approaching. He must have realised that if he was to have any kind of career in Scotland he would have to start soon. He had changed from the fine upstanding young doctor who had arrived in Zanzibar nearly nine years before. 'When you see me if ever you do, you will not know me, for I am now an old man, with white hair and beard,' he had written to his brother in 1873.[21] And he had glimpsed the changes that lay ahead for Zanzibar

– the scramble for Africa; the British East African empire that would arise out of the informal imperialism that Christie had witnessed. The way had been prepared in part by the naval tactics that he had so strongly opposed.

In May, 1874 James and Betsy Christie boarded a steamer for Natal, preferring the roundabout route home to a passage through the Suez Canal. Early in June they boarded the Royal Mail steamer *Kafir*, calling at Table Bay before the beginning of the long voyage to Southampton.[22]

CHAPTER 14

Out of Africa

MUCH HAD CHANGED in Glasgow during Christie's nine-year absence. The city was flourishing. A 'tidal wave of prosperity' had come surging in. Iron steamers were being hammered out in the Clyde yards, marine engines were being built and machine tools were produced for the local heavy industries. The population was growing – it was now well past the half-million mark. Most of the growth had been in the suburbs, with many of the older city parishes losing population to the newer districts, partly because of railway developments and the slum clearance programme initiated by the City Improvement Trust. It was a period of exceptional dislocation. The city had become outwardly mobile as the working classes moved to Govan or the fast-growing suburbs of Maryhill and Springburn and the middle-classes drifted towards the villas of the South side or terraces and crescents of the West End.[1] Glasgow University too had moved westwards to its commanding position on Gilmorehill, and the nearby Western Infirmary accepted its first patients within weeks of Christie's return to the city.

Glasgow's health and environmental problems, however, were still formidable. The City Improvement Trust had cleared the worst of the slums but the provision of new houses had been left entirely to the private sector, and not nearly enough had been built to prevent overcrowding elsewhere. Conditions in the more densely packed areas remained dire, with privies and even staircases being used as public urinals. The Saltmarket and Bridgegate were still squalid and disease-ridden. But at least Glasgow now had a full-time medical officer of health, the first to be appointed in Scotland. James Burn Russell, whom Christie had known a dozen years before in their Royal Infirmary days, had taken up his post in the Sanitary Office in Montrose Street about two years before Christie's return to Glasgow. Soon he set about gathering detailed statistical evidence to demonstrate the relation between living conditions and disease. The districts with the highest population densities, which were also the ones with the greatest number of occupants per room, had far higher death rates than other areas of the city. A quarter of the city's population lived in single ends, compared with 17 per cent in Edinburgh. These findings were to provide the statistical foundations for Russell's long and heroic battle to ameliorate terrible housing conditions through sanitary and environmental reform – a struggle which before the end of the century would make Glasgow renowned for its public health regime and Russell's name internationally recognised. It was a struggle in which Christie, too, would have a part to play.

If Glasgow had changed, so had Christie. He had left as a promising specialist in morbid psychology. He returned, grey-haired and moulded by his extraordinary African experiences, as an epidemiologist and authority on tropical diseases, quite widely known through his *Lancet* articles on cholera. Russell, who had previously been no more than an acquaintance, welcomed him warmly as a fellow-member of the public health fraternity. It was the beginning of a professional partnership and personal friendship that was to be of significance for both men, and for Glasgow. At this stage in their careers both were somewhat isolated. Russell had no assistant and no medical staff at his command – he was developing a strategy of working through the sanitary inspectors, though in theory he had no authority over them. Christie, having been cut off from the Glasgow medical world for almost a decade, lacked professional contacts.

The two men had much in common. Both were almost compulsive communicators; both were prolific and stylish writers on medical matters, although Christie for all his imaginative sweep and erudition could not quite touch Russell at his eloquent best. Both had highly analytical minds and a scientific approach to their work, and both were thoroughly at home with health statistics. Both took a broad, environmentally conscious approach to their work. Their views on public health matters were similar though not identical – Christie was the more radical of the two. Russell, like Christie, had a flair for medical detection – he would tramp round muddy farmsteads in search of clues to the origin of milk fever epidemics. He admired Christie's proficiency in inductive investigation and remarked that he had 'the patience and confident perseverance of the ant in accumulating his facts, and the skill of the true Baconian in marshalling them to a conclusion'. Temperamentally, too, there were some similarities. Russell, the younger by eight years, was an exceptionally shy man. Christie was less so, but was restrained and even guarded in manner except when giving vent to one of what Russell called his 'great spurts of utterances'. Before long the two were in frequent communication. As Russell later put it: 'Rarely did a week pass without . . . a visit and a short chat on something concerning the subject uppermost in both our minds.'[2] Over the years Christie would have a part to play in Russell's crusade against urban squalor, and their co-operation would have huge benefits for Christie's own work.

Although Christie was obviously committed to devoting the rest of his career to public health he seemed in no great hurry to find work. Zanzibar was still very much on his mind as he and his wife settled into their new flat in Sauchiehall Street, just outside the more fashionable Blythswood district (which had been largely colonised by doctors). During his first winter after his return he went through his Zanzibar notebooks, extracting everything relating to cholera epidemics with a view to comparing his clinical observations with those of other investigators. When this was finished he resumed his correspondence with Netten Radcliffe, of the London Epidemiological Society, who had instigated his researches into the origins of the cholera epidemics of East Africa.

Christie was aware that there was a missing link in his research into the 1869-70 epidemic – its precise track through Abyssinia. From the accounts of travellers and adventurers he had been able to establish that the disease had travelled southwards through Abyssinia but its exact course could not be plotted because of the anarchy and confusion in that war-torn land. But now Netten Radcliffe proved an invaluable contact. A Yorkshire man of Christie's own age, he was said to be an indifferent administrator who was 'happier when pursuing his own favourite avocation of collecting materials from every conceivable and inconceivable source concerning outbreaks of exotic diseases'. His ability to weave together isolated scraps of information into a coherent pattern, in much the same manner as Christie, had won him recognition as a historian of epidemiology.[3] He was able to send Christie the dates of the epidemic in Abyssinia, and when Christie studied the information he saw to his surprise that the epidemic of 1865 on the Somali coast – the one that had not reached Zanzibar because of the early onset of the monsoon – and the 1869-70 outbreak in Zanzibar were branches of the same epidemic, the great epidemic of 1865. It happened that about the same time the *Last Journals* of David Livingstone were published, providing precise information about the 'havoc' created by cholera in Manyuema country near Lake Tanganyika.

For Christie all this came as a total revelation: 'The great epidemic of 1864-71 appeared before me without a single missing link, so that I could almost imagine that I had seen the march of the disease throughout Africa.' [4]

It was then that he first thought of writing a book about the history of the epidemics, although he still doubted whether other people would find the subject interesting. He realised that the bare outline of the cholera tracks would make dull reading and would not reveal the laws regulating the propagation of the disease: the subject could be understood only in relation to the geography, ethnology, commercial connections, and tribal customs of the areas through which the disease had travelled. His aim was 'not to write a scientific treatise on the disease, but to note everything that I imagined had any reference to the propagation of epidemic cholera as observed by me in East Africa.' [5]

In his top flat near Charing Cross, in the middle of a district inhabited by fleshers, dyers, clothiers, glaziers and furriers, he set his sights on Africa and tracked the various cholera epidemics step-by-step in vivid detail. He wrote a stomach-churning description of the sanitary condition of Zanzibar, a gruesome personal account of the 1869-70 epidemic, and an exposition of how the disease had spread from Zanzibar north to the island of Socotra in the mouth of the Gulf of Aden, south to the mouth of the Zambezi, and west to Manyuema country, where Livingstone had spent his last days. He added a chapter on the role of the annual Mecca pilgrimage as a potent disseminator of the disease. Every caravan route, he maintained, had been at one time or other a cholera track; a single caravan had been known to lose more than a thousand men on its journey.

In a chapter that Christie clearly relished writing he dissected the theories of Dr James Bryden, statistical officer to the Government of India's Sanitary Commission, who maintained that cholera was an airborne disease propelled like a plague of locusts by monsoon currents. Bryden had argued that the 1869-70 epidemic in Zanzibar had arrived after the setting in of the north-west monsoon at the end of October, but Christie was able to demonstrate that cholera had been present in East Africa 'long before the first breath of the north-east monsoon of 1869 could possibly have reached that place.' He noted that Bryden's report on the epidemic failed to take full account of John Kirk's reports to the Government of India – and completely ignored Christie's own *Lancet* articles, although they had been commented on in the other medical journals. In the face of his authoritative analysis, underpinned by detailed references to dates and places, Bryden's vague theories completely evaporated, so Christie was able to conclude convincingly that 'Dr Bryden's "southern aerial epidemic highway" . . . has no existence; for the disease moved solely along the highways of human intercourse, and in certain definite relations to that intercourse.'[6] Later Christie's friend and fellow-epidemiologist James Burn Russell was to remark that his work caused 'the further discomfiture of those who called in the help of atmospheric currents and pandemic waves'.[7]

Christie also brought his researches to bear on the findings of the

International Sanitary Conference at Vienna in 1874, which had been in session just as he was travelling home from Africa. This was the fourth in a series of conferences convened by states with strong maritime interests which wished to regulate and control the anti-cholera initiatives of port authorities. International conferences on everything from telegraphic services to time zones were proliferating in the second half of the nineteenth century, although intensifying nationalism within the European states was an obstacle to accord: tactical compromises and alliances of expediency were the order of the day. The Vienna conference, like the previous sanitary summits, was divided between advocates and opponents of maritime quarantine.

The delegates – mainly doctors and sanitarians in the public service – were in unanimous agreement, however, that cholera was transmissable by human agency and that it could be spread by drinking water.[8] To Christie's satisfaction the delegates – from Britain, Russia, Egypt and about twenty Continental countries – were also agreed that the disease could not be carried for any distance by atmosphere alone, and that no epidemic had ever spread more quickly than human travel. His own researches, he felt justified in suggesting, 'fortified' the findings of the conference, 'the more important of which were that cholera is propagated by man, by water, and by personal effects'.

He wrote his book with enviable speed. It was published in 1876 by Macmillan. The reception was enthusiastic. 'No review can do proper justice to a book of this class,' enthused *The Lancet,* adding that it had 'filled up a hiatus in the history of cholera which had been a source of infinite blundering among epidemiologists'. The *London Medical Record* pronounced it 'a valuable contribution to our knowledge of the spread and propagation of cholera', and the *Practitioner* found the book 'readable and valuable quite apart from its special subject'.

The lay press was also full of praise. The *Glasgow Herald,* comparing the book with the writings of Richard Burton and Livingstone, found it full of valuable information on the geography, ethnology and trade of East Africa. The same qualities were highlighted by the *Geographical Magazine*, whose reviewer remarked that in addition to its medical importance the book painted a vivid picture of the mode of life of the inhabitants of Arabia and East Africa. The book also received a favourable mention in one of the reports of the medical officer of the Privy Council and Local Government Board, who thought that Christie's work was 'a unique example of the application of geographical research in the elucidation of an etiological question'.[9]

The book marked him out for attention and one of his colleagues remarked that 'from then on he took his place among the leading sanitary authorities of this country'. His profile was raised further when he began in the same year to edit the recently founded *Sanitary Journal for Scotland*. This work brought him into contact with most leading sanitarians in Britain and throughout Europe, the United States and India (where he was already well known because of his African connection). The journal was in a precarious state when Christie took it over. After only a few issues it had run up debts and lost its first editor. Christie soon invigorated the journal and, with his love of controversy, 'was always on the look out for something to commend, censure, or expound in his leaders'. As his friend James Burn Russell described it:

> Now he held up to scorn some parochial conclave
> discussing whether their sanitary inspector should get
> £5 or 50s; now he descended upon the middens and
> mire of some Gandercleuch. At one time it was a plea for
> rural sanitary reform; at another a cry for a
> reconstruction of the Central Authority. Always one was
> attracted by the clear, cold style, lance-like and
> unrelenting in controversy; unimpassioned, but
> impressive in exposition.[10]

Around the same time he found a more popular outlet for his writing talent through regular contributions to the *Globe Cyclopedia* on every variety of medical subject. Its editor, Christie's old student friend John Merry Ross, who was now senior English master at Edinburgh Royal High School, once recorded that none of his large team of learned contributors in science and the arts surpassed Christie in the precision and elegance of their literary work.

But what Christie needed was regular paid employment. At the end of 1876 he secured this when he became a dispensary (or out-patient) surgeon at the new Western Infirmary. Since the post was part-time Christie was free to look around for additional work. Early in 1877 an interesting opportunity arose with the death of one of Glasgow's Poor Law doctors. Under the Poor Law (Amendment) Act of 1845 the medical care of paupers in Scotland, who had hitherto been left largely to the private benevolence of doctors, became the responsibility of parochial boards elected by ratepayers and overseen by a central body, the Board of Supervision.[11] Christie was one of six applicants for the vacant part-time post in Broomielaw district, but despite the prestige he had gained from the recent publication of his book he was unsuccessful.[12] Robert Park, assistant superintendant at the Royal Infirmary and South-side practitioner, was given the job although his academic qualifications were less impressive than Christie's. Park remained in this post for thirty years and distinguished himself by a number of published papers.

The next job for which Christie applied could not have been more different – medical officer of health for the middle-class suburban burgh of Hillhead. Surprisingly, Glasgow had not yet annexed this district although there was no green space left between it and the city. After a rapid influx of population in the 1860s, as Glasgow's profess-ional and business classes pushed westwards across the River Kelvin, Hillhead had become a police burgh under the provisions of the Lindsay Act of 1862. This enabled its urban population to escape from the inefficient clutches of rural administration and also place themselves in a stronger bargaining position for the inevitable day when Glasgow would move to take over the area.[13] The tiny burgh, with a population of under 4000, was enlightened enough to adopt the Public Health (Scotland) Act of 1867, which obliged it to appoint a medical officer and a sanitary inspector. As their first Medical Officer of Health they had appointed James Dobbie, a well known local practitioner who resembled Christie in that he was described as 'unassuming and unobtrusive'. He had also had his share of adventure: as a young man he had been surgeon on an emigrant vessel sailing to New Zealand, and had returned by China and India to complete the world tour. His health was delicate and he was only 41 when he caught enteric fever during an epidemic in Hillhead and, in the words of one of his colleagues, 'succumbed to the toils of a laborious profession in our inhospitable climate'.[14] These were the toils that Christie, who had no shortage of experience of inhospitable climates, was appointed to take over in 1878.

CHAPTER 15
Hillhead

CHRISTIE took over not only James Dobbie's job but also his private practice and his rented town house at 2 Great Kelvin Terrace, Hillhead. Despite its imposing name Great Kelvin Terrace was less grand than many properties further west; it was in fact merely the last block of Bank Street before Great Western Road, for this was a time when streets were being subdivided into crescents and terraces with impressive names. Bank Street, however, had a certain importance since it led from Great Western Road to the university. Queen Victoria's landau passed along the street in 1888 when she was on her way to Glasgow's first International Exhibition in Kelvingrove Park, but given the views he had once expressed on the monarch, it is unlikely that Christie rushed to the door or window to give a loyal wave.[1] On other occasions Bank Street was enlivened by street musicians and other entertainers, including an aged Italian with a barrel organ and monkey, a man with a piano organ which churned out the 'Marseillaise', and a German band.

The Christies' house was at the end of the terrace, near the recently built Cooper's grocery emporium with its distinctive clock tower.[2] The practice was run from the house. The presence of a doctor was advertised, according to custom in Hillhead, by a red lamp at the gate. At dusk the lamp would be lit by a man bearing a pole with a flame at the end, a ritual that constantly fascinated the small boy waiting at the window of the house next door. The boy, whose father was a well known tobacco manufacturer, was later to win fame as J.J. Bell, author of the 'Wee Magreegor' adventures and also of published reminiscences in which his Hillhead boyhood days are described. Christie was not the Bells' doctor but he occasionally came to the rescue after family mishaps – as when one of the boys cut himself while dancing in a wash-hand basin until it broke.[3]

Christie's practice could not have been more different from his multi-ethnic Zanzibar one. Hillhead was predominantly middle class. On weekdays a procession of soberly garbed men emerged from the side streets and high terraces to board horse-drawn trams from Great Western Road into the city. On Sundays the scenes were described by a witness as 'almost spectacular in their respectability', with large numbers of church-goers taking to the streets in best bonnets and black silk hats.[4] Christie and his wife were sometimes among them for, despite some residual contacts with the Evangelical Union, he liked to hear his old student friend John Service preach at Hyndland Church. But sometimes as he watched the passing scene he must have remembered Zanzibar City's chaotic streets and the corpses on the beach.

Even the contrast between Hillhead and Glasgow was sharp. Hillhead's middle-class residents lived in a different world from the inhabitants of the city slums. When Christie took up his MOH appointment in 1878 Glasgow was going through a particularly bad spell. The local economy was in recession: soup was ladled out in the night asylums and the unemployed were put to work clearing snow or working in the docks and parks at a ha'penny a day. The effects of the economic downturn were compounded by the City of Glasgow Bank failure of 1878. The City Improvement Trust abandoned its building programme and attempted to patch up the properties that it had acquired for demolition, soon becoming Glasgow's biggest slum landlord. The Saltmarket and similar areas still had their typhus nests, while Glasgow's smoky atmosphere and freezing fogs made lung diseases the scourge of the city. James Burn Russell remarked that Glasgow, which had the purest drinking water in the kingdom, had the most impure air. It was in his words 'a semi-asphyxiated city'.

Hillhead, in contrast, was such a healthy place that it might be thought that a medical officer would have had little to do. The streets were kept clean, household refuse was collected daily, and the dairy farms were hygienically run. There were no smoky factories – just some smithies, farriers' premises and joiners' workshops. Yet even a well-heeled Victorian suburb had its health problems. Germs were no respecters of municipal boundaries, and although the era of adult infectious diseases had waned, childhood diseases such as measles, chickenpox and whooping cough were still rife. Hillhead was exposed not only to the communicable diseases of the city but also sometimes to its polluted air – as in Glasgow, lung disease was the leading cause of death. The countryside too posed threats. The burgh was dependent for its milk supplies on a variety of far-flung farms as its own exemplary dairy farms could not supply all its needs. These farms were almost beyond the reach of public health laws and their standards of hygiene were low. Enteric fever and other diseases were deeply entrenched in the rural mud. Hillhead's sanitary officials made frequent expeditions to the countryside to track down the source of outbreaks of these milk fevers. Christie, meanwhile, continued his crusade for rural sanitary reform in the pages of the *Sanitary Journal.*

Hillhead also had its share of problems peculiar to middle-class communities. The authorities had difficulty in finding places to put public lavatories. Iron urinals were constructed in one residential street, taken away again after local protests, re-erected in a nearby lane, removed after more protests, and finally deposited on the burgh's own ground behind the new burgh hall, where they remained a target for complaints. (Nimbyism is no new phenomenon.) There were also problems of the Commissioners' own making. Although they were generally progressive in public health matters, there were times when their standards slipped – for example they saw nothing wrong with allowing the newly built Glasgow Academy to install earth closets.[5]

One way or another Christie was not short of work. As was to be expected he was a sharp observer of Hillhead's tribal customs; his monthly and annual reports reveal much about the ways of a middle-class Victorian burgh on Glasgow's doorstep and allow comparisons to be made with other places.[6] The reports recorded all births and deaths, age at death and cause of death. Lung diseases – including bronchitis, pneumonia and pulmonary consumption – were the leading causes, usually accounting for about a third of deaths. Sometimes the reported cause was rather vague – 'general debility', 'old age' – and occasionally it was something unusual, such as suicide, a fall from a window, or a drowning in the Kelvin. Once a dead man and a dying man were found together in a house, having apparently taken an overdose of horse medicine.

Christie was constantly comparing Hillhead's statistics with those of other places. In his report for 1886, a year in which the burgh had been free from epidemic disease, he claimed that Hillhead's death rate of 9.22 per 1000 was the lowest in the UK, beating Plumstead's 13 per 1000, the lowest rate for any of London's sanitary districts. Hillhead's infant mortality in the same year was 33 per 1000 compared with Edinburgh's 136 per 1000. In this connection Christie also commented that the 'normal rate for the upper classes' had been estimated at 64.1.[7] Comparisons with Glasgow's statistics showed some striking contrasts. In 1890 the burgh's death rate was 12 per 1000 compare with Glasgow's 22 (which itself represented a sharp fall during the 1880s). In the same year mortality from infectious diseases in the burgh was only 6.09 per cent compared with 16.11 per cent for the principal towns of Scotland. The figures would have been even more impressive if Christie had not subtracted Hillhead's 1428 servants from the total population of 8264 on the grounds that, with their permanent homes elsewhere, they contributed almost nothing to the burgh's birth and death statistics.[8]

Hillhead's good health record obviously reflected its socio-economic and geographical advantages: it was far enough from the city to escape the worst environmental problems, near enough to take advantage of hospitals and municipal services. Yet its progressive and efficient public health regime also played a part. Christie was constantly urging the authorities to adopt innovative methods and equipment, such as a 'destructor' in which the burgh's rubbish would be burned. It was significant, too, that Hillhead was among the first

Scottish burghs to adopt the Infectious Diseases (Notification) Act of 1889, which compelled doctors to notify cases of infectious disease to the medical officer – a measure which Christie had long argued should be universally compulsory rather than adoptive; he had in fact tried for years to operate an early warning system.[9] He also felt frustrated by the associated bye-laws recommended by the Board of Supervision (Scotland's central health authority) which empowered only the chief sanitary inspector, and not the medical officer, to investigate the diseases that were notified. He argued strongly against the adoption of the bye-laws,[10] no doubt after lengthy discussions with his friend James Burn Russell, who had experienced a similar anomaly in Glasgow.

The Hillhead situation was particularly ridiculous in that the sanitary inspector, Thomas Simpson, was a policeman who had found himself in public health work by chance. That said, Simpson appears to have done his work vigorously and conscientiously and certainly cracked down hard on anyone who broke the public health laws, once threatening a woman and her doctor with prosecution because they had sent a domestic servant with suspected German measles to hospital in a hired cab. He also ordered the police to give daily reports on any filth or rubbish being dumped within the burgh, so that it could be quickly removed. But despite his commanding personality, which comes across in his sanitary reports, he did defer to Christie when, for example, instructed to investigate defective drainage.[11]

As Hillhead's medical officer Christie developed a close working partnership with James Burn Russell, Glasgow's MOH. The regular chats of these like-minded men must have made Russell feel less isolated than he might otherwise have done. An example of their collaboration occurred in the summer of 1880 when Christie was asked by the parish authorities to investigate an outbreak of enteric fever in the new working-class district of Possilpark beyond Glasgow's northern boundary. He conferred with Russell, who had been investigating similar outbreaks within the city, and when they compared notes they saw a pattern that pointed to a common cause. The outbreak was traced first to a Glasgow wholesale milk dealer and then to one of the farms supplying him. Those customers of the dealer who escaped the disease were found to drink buttermilk or take only a tiny drop of milk in their tea. Christie remarked that the whole investigation had something of the precision of a laboratory experiment.[12]

Christie also had another outlet for his views. In 1879 he was appointed lecturer in hygiene and public health at Anderson's Medical College, teaching the first systematic course in this subject in Scotland. His introductory lecture, delivered just a week after his fiftieth birthday, consisted of a wide-ranging survey of the history of sanitary science from Mosaic law onwards, taking in everything from the plague at Marseilles to the sweating sickness that broke out after the Battle of Bosworth. Sanitary science, he told his audience, had made no advances in Europe from the fall of the Roman Empire until recent times, for the aqueducts and sewers destroyed by the Goths were allowed to remain in a state of disrepair. Quarantine laws would never be enough, he added, for it was insanitary conditions that gave epidemics all their potency.[13] Possibly as he spoke he had a vision of Zanzibar's cesspools.

Christie seems to have been an indifferent lecturer, his style being 'almost too classical'. He had little previous experience of public speaking. But he was innovative in his methods, introducing specialist speakers to cover the various topics in his course. He also broke new ground by giving public health lectures to students at Glasgow Dental Hospital, which started life as part of Anderson's Medical College.[14] He was said to be 'beloved by his students and colleagues for his unfailing kindness' and was very much in sympathy with the class of students for whom Anderson's College existed. 'I have very great sympathy with students who have brains but very little money to enable them to advance,' he once told a colleague. 'But if there are any I pity more it is those who have money but very little brains.'[15]

After four years as public health lecturer he applied for the post of Professor of the Practice of Medicine at Anderson's, but was passed over in favour of Samson Gemmell, his famously erudite colleague at the Western Infirmary Dispensary whose name is still linked with child health in Glasgow. Soon afterwards, however, Christie successfully applied for the post of Professor of Physiology at Anderson's, though he continued also to lecture in public health and hygiene.[16]

He was now part of Glasgow's medical establishment. As well as editor of the *Sanitary Journal* he was a Fellow of the Faculty of Physicians and Surgeons of Glasgow (and its examiner in arts) and a member of the Medico-Chirurgical Society of Glasgow. He became secretary of the newly formed Glasgow and West of Scotland branch of the British Medical Association and secretary of the sanitary section of the Philosophical Society of Glasgow. More exotically, he was also the Epidemiological Society of London's secretary for the Indian Ocean and East Africa, a corresponding member of the Medical and Physical Society of Bombay and an associate of the French Society of Hygiene. As an authority on sanitary questions he was often called as an expert witness or referee in legal cases.

Hillhead might have seemed a limited sphere of operations after Africa. But he constantly looked beyond the burgh boundaries. His influence was felt far beyond Hillhead. He was a natural campaigner, a lover of controversy and argument. In his lectures, his *Sanitary Journal* editorials and his prolific writings he unceasingly promoted the case for public health reform. A constant theme was the need for stronger Scottish health legislation. He deplored the feebleness of the Public Health (Scotland) Act of 1867, which was merely permissive legislation and in his view 'tentative'.[17] He criticised the Infectious Diseases (Notification) Act for the same reason. He thought that Scotland should have a central health board armed with power to enforce sanitary measures. He argued strongly for the establishment of free dispensaries (or out-patient clinics) for people who failed to qualify for Poor Law support but whose resources might be strained by, for example, dependant relatives. This would be to the general good, he pointed out, because it would improve the health of the working class 'who are the backbone and the basis upon which the prosperity of the country must rest'. Such a scheme would also allow more extensive medical surveillance of the population and make the registration of communicable diseases a practical possibility. In this matter Christie was more radical than James Burn Russell, who preferred the idea of simply extending charities to benefit the same class.[18]

After arguing successfully for a disinfection apparatus to be set up in Hillhead he used his speech at the opening ceremony in 1881 to call for a cordon of similar disinfection stations to encircle the city.[19] He denounced the many local authorities who were either too apathetic or too parsimonious to take effective measures for disinfection. 'The most expensive mode of dealing with isolated cases of infection is to allow them to develop into epidemics without the expenditure of a single farthing,' he pointed out.

He also criticised local authorities in small towns and rural districts for failing to co-operate over clean water supplies – and, in a recommendation that would nowadays be described as 'green', he advocated the greater use of rainwater falling on slated rural roofs (urban rainwater, he added, would be too polluted for this purpose). He attacked local authorities as well for being too mean to pay their medical officers and sanitary inspectors more than paltry amounts, typically around £5 a year. He damned local authorities in small towns, and particularly their registrars, for not supplying medical officers and sanitary inspectors with the returns of births and deaths. As editor of the *Sanitary Journal* he received minutely detailed monthly reports from Michigan – 'but the statistics of the Clyde watering places cannot be procured, probably because they existed only in the books of the local registrar and if known to the local authority suppressed, or made known only when the death rate was very low.'

He also warned that the watering places of Scotland would never attract many visitors until they improved their methods of sewage disposal, which in many instances was 'a disgrace'. By the same token he warned that Glasgow businessmen who at that time were increasingly attracted by the idea of living outside the city would not go to places which lacked reasonably good sanitary arrangements. 'A complete sanitary system is, in such cases, a source of wealth, and not a useless sentimental expenditure,' he maintained, in a shrewd appeal to the pocket.

Slums, he pointed out, were to be found in the country as well as in large cities. Once, on holiday with a medical friend, he took the opportunity not only to examine the sanitary arrangements of a small town but also to demand entry to a common lodging house where tramps and vagrants were accommodated overnight. 'The proprietress seemed at first to be rather suspicious about me,' he later recalled; 'but she evidently concluded that I was an official from the Board of Supervision when I told her to open the doors and show me the rooms of her house.' Inside he found that the facilities provided for female factory workers included galvanised iron or zinc pails without seats. Since the house had no connection with the sewage system the pails were tipped onto a huge rubbish heap near the building. Christie also examined the pig sty, where the animals were wading up to their bellies in semi-liquid refuse from the adjoining slaughterhouse. 'A more disgusting sight I have never witnessed,' commented Christie, who had seen plenty of disgusting sights in Zanzibar.[20]

All this added up to a sustained campaign for sanitary innovation and reform – a rural crusade to complement James Burn Russell's bigger battle against urban squalor and ill health. (Christie perhaps had wry reservations about Russell's stated aim of making the city as healthy as the countryside, although Russell, too, recognised the urgent need for rural reform.) The co-operation between the two of them was a crucial part of Christie's contribution to Scottish public health reform. Neighbouring burghs often asked Russell for help with their sanitation problems, and the pressures on him must often have been eased by the opportunity to involve Christie in such questions. He also shared his deep concerns about the sanitary state of dairy farms supplying urban areas with milk. Russell appreciated Christie's enthusiasm for sanitary reform and the investigative skills that he had developed in Zanzibar. In 1880 when Russell was granted two months' leave of absence, his health broken by the stress of the enteric fever epidemic and by the burden of recent widowhood, Christie was the natural choice to become acting MOH for Glasgow.[21]

The Scottish part of Christie's career was therefore no mere coda to Zanzibar, nor was it entirely separate from his African experience. From Zanzibar's cholera epidemic of 1869-70 he had learned the vital lesson that, as he once put it, 'the most efficacious mode of arresting an epidemic is to strangle it at birth.' This medical message was a constant theme in all his writing, usually accompanied by the well-judged argument that speedy action was much less costly than delay. Sometimes he cited his Zanzibar experience to emphasise the point.

Zanzibar had certainly not been forgotten at 2 Great Kelvin Terrace. As well as writing to his old Swahili teacher, Mohammed, Christie kept in touch with H.M. Stanley, writing to commiserate with him when he was running into heavy criticism in England. In his reply Stanley described Christie as 'a true friend' and assured him that his friendship was reciprocated. Later, when Stanley was making a whirlwind tour of Scotland, Christie invited him to lunch, but Stanley had to catch a train to Dunfermline and could only suggest that Christie should come to his hotel to 'take a glass of wine and talk Swahili to my boy.'[22]

In the midst of dealing with Hillhead's disinfection problems and its suspect milk supplies Christie still made time to write about tropical medicine. He contributed a chapter on tropical skin diseases to Professor Thomas McCall Anderson's *Treatise on Diseases of the Skin*, describing among other disorders Delhi boil, leprosy, yaws, fungus foot of India and pellagra.[23] He extended his range by writing a paper on yellow fever in the United States. And, drawing on his Zanzibar experiences, he wrote a paper on dengue fever which was read in shortened form at the seventh International Medical Congress in London in the summer of 1881. This vast congress, attended by more than 3000 delegates from some 70 countries, has been credited with ushering medical science on to the public stage.[24] The growing interest in tropical medicine resulting from sharpening imperial rivalries must have ensured a good audience for Christie's paper, especially since dengue fever had spread alarmingly in the later 1870s. The paper described the epidemic that had followed after the 1869-70 cholera epidemic in Zanzibar and then, speculating on its aetiology, linked it with both germ theory and Darwin's evolutionary doctrine. Dengue fever, he suggested, was perhaps a hybrid disease arising from modifications to the cholera germ produced by human decomposition. He seemed to be groping towards some concept of germ mutation, but was hopelessly off track in connecting it with dengue fever. Early in the twentieth century it would be demonstrated that the vector was a variety of mosquito, though the actual virus was not identified until the 1940s. But at least Christie recognised that dengue fever spread along lines of human communication, particularly shipping lines.[25] He had begun to amass material on this subject with a view to writing a companion volume to his cholera book.[26]

More important than any of these later tropical writings were the lessons that Christie had brought back with him from East Africa – not least the imperative need to tackle potential epidemics right at the outset, in the rural muck of Ayrshire or Renfrewshire just as much as in the cesspools and shama wells of Zanzibar. 'No man did more . . . to sustain the waning cause of sanitation in Scotland,' as James Burn Russell was later to write. Yet his contribution to Scottish public health is as sadly unremembered as his cholera work.

CHAPTER 16
End Game

W HEN CHRISTIE celebrated his sixtieth birthday in May, 1889, he had some cause for satisfaction. The climate for public health reform had improved during the 1880s. The pacemaker was Glasgow. The local economy was booming again. The International Exhibition of 1888 had inspired a new mood of public confidence. The city was about to enter an era of astonishing municipal enterprise, with the Town Council (soon to evolve into Glasgow Corporation) reaching out and taking control of everything from trams to markets. James Burn Russell, armed by now with a great array of statutory powers, and enjoying an international reputation, was right at the centre of this development. Working with his allies on the Town Council's health committee he had initiated local police bills which gave him the authority to condemn unhealthy houses.

Glasgow's death rate fell more rapidly than that of other Scottish cities. The sanitary office had evolved into a modern public health department, concerned with everything from building regulations to food standards.[1] With Glasgow's dairy inspectors penetrating as far as Biggar, the benefits were felt far beyond the city boundaries. Russell, like Christie, recognised that the unreformed state of rural public health was a threat to urban areas. In the absence of an effective Scottish public health authority he issued a memorandum on the sanitary requirements of dairy farms to all suppliers of milk to Glasgow.

Christie himself could claim much credit for the improved climate for public health. For years he had agitated for reform in the pages of the *Sanitary Journal* and in his lectures. For a long time his message went unheeded but by the end of the 1880s change was in the air. One leading MOH referred to 'the present stir in sanitary matters'. Christie had become a rallying point for reformers and it was not surprising that in the summer of 1898 he was the representative selected by the West of Scotland branch of the British Medical Association to go to London to interview the Lord Advocate on the sanitary clauses of the Local Government (Scotland) Bill, which was then in the pipeline. The result was that the legislation was considerably strengthened. Sanitary measures which had been merely optional in the Bill were made compulsory in the Act.

The new elected county councils, which were set up under the Act, were compelled to appoint full-time medical officers and sanitary inspectors. The Act, which passed in 1889, was therefore a piece of landmark legislation for Scottish public health as well as local government. According to one of Chistie's colleagues, it at last provided Scotland with 'a proper sanitary service'.[2] Medical men who had previously shown little interest in sanitary work stepped forward now that there was a prospect of work in this field. Courses on public health began to be offered in universities and colleges.

Christie was widely acknowledged to have played a key role in this reform. Not only had he argued his case successfully with the Lord Advocate, but he had also educated public opinion to a degree that made it impossible for the legislators to reject his proposals.[3] And when the reforms became law, later in the same year, he still felt he had work to do. He was not in the mood to sit back and watch others implement the new measures. He wanted to be in on the action himself. At the age of 61, he applied for the post of Medical Officer of Health for Renfrewshire. This position would provide the ideal base for the implementation of the radical reforms which he had done so much to bring about.

In any case, his time as Hillhead's MOH was running out. The burgh's independent status was under grave threat, and with it Christie's MOH post. Glasgow had long wished to take over the surrounding middle-class burghs and districts, with their high rateable values and their building land. There was bitterness at their free use of city amenities, particularly parks, which were situated close to the suburbs. Various attempts at annexation failed in the face of fierce local resistance, but by 1890 it was becoming obvious that there would be no stopping the mighty municipality. Russell was among those strongly favouring a boundary extension, which would also mean the expansion of his public health empire.

Opposition within the independent burghs was beginning to founder. Annexationists gained the majority in Hillhead Commission. Public opinion in the burgh was becoming bitterly divided. Many people were won over by Glasgow's argument that better services would more than compensate for higher rates in the event of a municipal take-over. At a time when the fear of mob violence was widespread a property-conscious community was particularly attracted by the prospect of more efficient policing and fire-fighting services.[4] Edinburgh's influential MOH, Henry Littlejohn, claimed that small authorities were unable to afford enough modern sanitary equipment, adding that although Hillhead was one of the best small burghs he had seen, its best was not good enough. An Annexation Bill was drawn up in 1890 but after disagreement over which burghs should be excluded the House of Lords threw it out. Nevertheless it must have been obvious to everyone, not least Christie, that this was a mere stay of execution. Hence the added attraction of fresh – or unfresh – fields in Renfrewshire.

No other candidate for the post can have mustered such an impressive array of backers. Christie accompanied his application with testimonials from all the leading MOHs in Scotland and also from two of the most celebrated public health reformers of the nineteenth century: Edwin Chadwick and John Simon. Chadwick, the author of the seminal report on the sanitary condition of the British labouring classes, described Christie as being foremost 'in the perception of sanitary principles' while Simon, former medical officer of the Board of Health, acknowledged how Christie had assisted his department by providing information 'of permanent value' on East African cholera.

Despite this high-powered support Christie failed to get the post. It went instead to a much younger man, Dr A. Campbell Munro, a 37-year-old Edinburgh University graduate with a science degree in public health who was MOH for South Shields and Jarrow-on-Tyne.[5] It is doubtful in any case whether Christie would have been able to make much of such a job. By the time the Renfrewshire appointment was announced in the autumn of 1890 his health had began to fail. He developed cardiac problems and around the turn of the year was laid low by attacks of angina which were so violent that it seemed unlikely that he would ever resume work. A fire was lit in his bedroom and, with a paraffin lamp at the head of his bed, he went on with his writing, finding that he could write with a pencil in bed as easily and more comfortably than at his desk. But he was distracted by his wife's apparently distressed state. 'Mrs C. has been in a state of the deepest contrition and despondency today and has been imploring me all day,' he wrote to his brother Andrew in Kilmarnock in late November.[6] In the same month he altered his will so that his wife would not inherit his estate but would receive an annual income from Andrew Christie.

He surprised people by recovering from his bout of illness. As one of his colleagues put it, 'his naturally calm temperament came to his aid and he rallied.' New complications began to affect him in the spring and for a while the outlook again seemed hopeless, but again he improved and in the summer and autumn was 'seen going about and conducting examinations in Glasgow or Edinburgh as if little or nothing were amiss'. But his friend James Burn Russell observed with concern 'the whitening hair, the haggard face, the tottering step.' Russell was also sad to see that the lengthening shadow of a declining sun' was being cast over the pages of the *Sanitary Journal*, which had diminished in vigour in recent issues.[7]

By the time winter set in fresh complications were confining Christie mainly to the house, particularly in foggy weather. News of the bitter squabbling that marked the last days of Hillhead burgh must have reached Great Kelvin Terrace. Sticks were banged on the floor during angry meetings and men rose shouting from their seats.[8] Finally the annexationists won the day and Hillhead was among the six police burghs to agree to be absorbed into the city in November, 1891, almost doubling the size of Glasgow and adding more than 90,000 to the population. Guarantees of generous rating concessions for five years had eased the local pain. Burgh officials, of course, lost their jobs. Christie was among those who began to sue for compensation.

He outlived Hillhead by only a few weeks. Betsy Christie was present when he died from cardiac failure at Great Kelvin Terrace on the second day of 1892.

He was buried in Kilmarnock.

CHAPTER 17

Christie in Retrospect: East Africa and West End

There never was anyone who had a more hearty, enthusiastic, unselfish interest in sanitary affairs, both scientific and administrative.

James Burn Russell

JAMES CHRISTIE'S obituarists acknowledged the importance of both his cholera work and his contributions to Scottish public health. The *Sanitary Journal* noted that after the publication of his book on the origins of the East African epidemics he had taken his place among the leading sanitarians of Britain.[1] James Burn Russell wrote that no man had done more than Christie 'to sustain the waning cause of sanitation in Scotland'.[2] *The Lancet* claimed that his views on medical education were much in advance of his time.[3] His erudition, cultured mind and qualities of perseverance were frequently noted. It was widely agreed that he was restrained and somewhat dignified in manner but kindly to friends, colleagues and students, and possessed of a fund of genial humour. Speaking in his calm and precise but emphatic manner he had always, it was remarked, commanded attention in meetings or debate. But, as Russell put it, anything like double-dealing, pretence or humbug 'stirred him up into great spurts of utterances'.

The obituaries also acknowledged his shortcomings – he was not a model lecturer, particularly in the case of less talented students, who struggled to understand him. Nor was he a model GP, at least in the estimation of one colleague who observed that 'his literary tastes and unobtrusive manners kept him back, as compared with others, in the whirl of practice, so that he found time for the cultivation of other work, for which perhaps he had more special aptitude.' It was certainly that 'other work' which was his main legacy.

Christie's professional life had been remarkably diverse, but there were continuities amid its sudden and unpredictable changes of direction. Even when moving on to something new he kept abreast of his former interests. In Glasgow he continued to write prolifically about tropical diseases and to amass material for a book on dengue fever. He even kept up his early interest in psychological medicine, dating from his Gartnavel days in the early 1860s. The tidy, well-heeled, church-going burgh of Hillhead could not have provided a sharper contrast to Zanzibar town, with its cesspits and squalid lanes, yet there were common threads between the two parts of Christie's career. His public health work in Scotland was strongly influenced by his African experiences, which led him to insist on the utter importance of stamping out infectious diseases before they reached epidemic level – a priority that applied to milk fevers and childhood infections just as much as to cholera. It was this background that made him such a valuable ally of James Burn Russell, bringing about a collaboration that was an essential part of Christie's contribution to public health reform.

In Zanzibar he had been an unorthodox member of the medical profession. Most young doctors who went to Africa at that time were attached to church missions. Christie, too, was a member of a mission but earned his living from private practice and was ahead of his time in treating Arabs and Indians and also African surgical cases. It was not until much later in the century that medicine as a colonial career began in East Africa, and even then health care for many years was provided exclusively for westerners.[4] Christie was also at odds with the emerging colonial ethos in a broader sense, strongly disapproving of the British consulate's attempts to tighten its grip on the still nominally independent sultanate of Zanzibar. Christie could almost be described as an anti-colonial doctor, and it was significant that he decided to head for home at a time when he could clearly foresee the coming European scramble for Africa, though this was not the only reason for his decision.

On his return to Scotland he became a recognised epidemiologist and a member of the Glasgow medical establishment but was still no great supporter of the status quo. He remained radical in his thinking – going further than James Burn Russell by, for example, advocating free out-patient clinics for people who narrowly failed to qualify for Poor Relief and arguing that this would improve the health of the working classes, who were the backbone of the nation. Characteristically, he declared himself in sympathy with the youths of limited means who attended his classes at Anderson's Medical College, preferring, as he put it, students with brains but no money to those with money but no brains.

To judge by the tributes of his friends the testy and impatient side of his personality was less in evidence than it had been in Zanzibar. Yet despite his restrained and polite manner his 'great spurts of utterances' seem to have continued in his later life. So, certainly, did the restless energy, intellectual curiosity and capacity for perseverance that had been the driving force behind his extraordinary book on the origins of East Africa's cholera epidemics, the supreme achievement of his life. To the end of his days he remained Christie of Zanzibar.

POSTSCRIPT: KILMARNOCK AND ZANZIBAR

AFTER HER HUSBAND'S DEATH Betsy Christie moved round the corner to Great Western Road and lived on for another dozen years. She too was buried in Kilmarnock, where the Christie family gravestones may still be seen. Christie's brother Andrew continued in his ironmongery business and was lucky to escape prosecution when a gunpowder explosion in the shop killed an assistant and caused mayhem in the street outside (an apprentice had been experimenting with the powder when the master was out of the shop). Andrew Christie's son later carried on the business, which is still remembered in Kilmarnock. Andrew Christie's daughter married an Ardrossan journalist and their own daughter inherited the letters written by James Christie in Zanzibar; and presumably because she was the last of the Christies she bequeathed them to a friend from her student days at Newnham College, Cambridge, who in turn donated them to Cambridge University. They are now in the archives of the university library.

In the closing years of his life Christie had seen his predictions for East Africa come true. European, and particularly German, interest in the area intensified in the 1880s and the Treaty of Berlin in 1885 marked the beginning of the scramble for Africa. Five years later, as part of an agreement with Germany (which received Heligoland in compensation) Zanzibar was declared a British protectorate. The Sultan was retained as a puppet ruler. This arrangement did not always work smoothly: British marines bombarded the Sultan's palace when an unfriendly candidate tried to take over during a succession struggle in the 1890s. But the protectorate lasted for three-quarters of a century, with the last of the sultans being overthrown in a violent revolution soon after Zanzibar became independent in 1963. Zanzibar united with the former Tanganyika to become the United Republic of Tanzania, retaining its own president and a considerable degree of autonomy. The narrow, crooked streets of Zanzibar City, now known as Stone Town, are much as they were in Christie's day (minus the filth and smells), although conservationists worry about the possible effects of Zanzibar's growing tourist industry.

Christie's pioneering work on cholera, though forgotten in Glasgow, is remembered by at least some people in East Africa, and his writing is sometimes quoted in guidebooks to the region. On a recent visit to Zanzibar I was able to gather information about him from sources outside as well as within the state archives, sometimes gaining new perspectives on aspects of his activities. The East African historian Professor Abdul Sheriff, now based on Zanzibar, told me that Christie deserved credit for having recognised that the naval tactics used by Britain to suppress the slave trade in West Africa were the wrong ones for East Africa, where slavery had long been part of the culture. A more benign view of the British navy's role, however, was taken at an English-language service at the Anglican Cathedral, whose foundation stone was laid on the site of the old slave market not long before Christie left Zanzibar. Bishop John Ramadhani, whose grandfather was a freed slave, offered thanks for the navy's efforts to end the trade.

A document in Zanzibar State Archives had indicated that the remains of Captain Fraser's old sugar factory, where Christie had once spent many unhappy hours struggling with accounts in several currencies, could still be seen at Mkokotoni. One Sunday afternoon I set off with a friend to find it. The taxi in which we were travelling was stopped at a police checkpoint and our guide was detained while the police attempted to find out why we were heading for such an untouristy place. Christie's journeys to Mkokotoni on horseback must have been more straightforward. At our destination we found a village surrounded by acres of rough, uncultivated land. There seemed no hope whatever of finding the remains of the sugar factory, but when our guide approached a row of men sitting on a bench one of them rose to his feet, beaming. He was Mshamera Chum Kombo, the local school teacher and a graduate of Dar-es-Salaam University – and he knew all about Christie's friend Captain Fraser. He then spent several hours guiding us round the former sugar plantation, showing us the remains of the factory and of the house on Pale Hill where Fraser had once stayed. Once again, local knowledge provided a slightly different perspective. Fraser was something of a hero to Mshamera Chum Kombo because he had introduced modern technology to the area.

So James Christie is not quite forgotten in Zanzibar.

Christie of Zanzibar

NOTES

Abbreviations

AC   Andrew Christie

JC   James Christie

GCA   Glasgow City Archives and Special Collections, the Mitchell Library, Glasgow, GB243

GMJ   *Glasgow Medical Journal*

NLS   National Library of Scotland

SJ   *The Sanitary Journal*

ZSA   Zanzibar State Archives

Preface

1 James Christie, *Cholera Epidemics in East Africa: An Account of the Several Diffusions of the Disease in that Country from 1821 till 1872* (London, 1876).

2 J.N P. Davies, 'James Christie and the Cholera Epidemics of East Africa', *East African Medical Journal*, January 1959, 36 (1), 1 - 6.

3 Kessinger Publishing's Rare Reprints.

4 Christopher Hamlin, *Cholera:the Biography* (Oxford, 2009), pp. 61-3, 75.

Chapter 1

1 A.V. Christie, *Brass Tacks and a Fiddle* (Privately printed, 1943. Dick Institute, Kilmarnock), pp. 9-11.

2 Christie, *Brass Tacks,* p. 12.

3 William Proudfoot, 'The Parish of Strathaven, July 1835' in the *The New Statistical Account of Scotland*: Lanarkshire (Edinburgh, 1841).

4 Proudfoot, Parish of Strathaven.

5 Christie, *Brass Tacks,* pp. 13 - 14.

Chapter 2

1 James Ross, *A History of Congregational Independency in Scotland* (Glasgow, 1900), p. 150.

2 William Adamson, *The Life of the Rev. James Morison* (London, 1898), p. 242

3 JC to AC, May 23, 1869. Copies of letters from Zanzibar, etc,. 1865-73, unpublished, Cambridge University Library, Add MS.8163. Extracts form the letters are by permission of the Syndics of the Cambridge University Library. (All the letters are to Christie's brother Andrew.)

4 Adamson, *Life of Morison.* p. 60.

5 Adamson, *Life of Morison.* p. 83

6 Adamson, *Life of Morison.* p. 143.

7 After a prolonged dispute about the right to nominate ministers, a large number of the clergy broke away from the Church of Scotland in 1843. Under the leadership of Thomas Chalmers they formed the Free Church of Scotland which asserted the right of congregations to appoint ministers, not landlords or other patrons.

8 Fergus Ferguson, *A History of the Evangelical Union* (Glasgow, 1876), p. 280.

9 Ross, *Congregational Independency,* p. 153.

10 Adamson, *Life of Morison,* p. 247.

11 Adamson, *Life of Morison,* pp. 246 - 7.

12 William D. McNaughton, *The Scottish Congregational*

Ministry, 1794 - 1993 (Glasgow, 1993); W. Innes Addison, *The Matriculation Albums of the University of Glasgow from 1728 to 1858* (Glasgow, 1913), p. 488; Addison, *A Roll of the graduates of the University of Glasgow, 1727 - 1897.*

13 1851 Census.

Chapter 3

1 H.A.L. Fisher, *James Bryce,* Vol. 1 (London, 1927), pp. 22 - 25.

2 Robert D. Anderson, *Education and Opportunity in Victorian Scotland: Schools and Universities,* 2nd ed. (Edinburgh, 1989), p. 308; Anne Crowther and Marguerite Dupree, 'The Invisible General Practitioner: the Careers of Scottish Medical Students in the Late Nineteenth Century', *Bulletin of the History of Medicine,* 1966, 70, p.397.

3 David Murray, *Memories of the Old College of Glasgow* (Glasgow, 1927), pp. 571, 580.

4 Murray, *Memories,* p. 571.

5 Murray, *Memories,* pp. 75 and 587n.

6 William Adamson, *The Life of the Rev. James Morison* (London, 1898), p. 338.

Chapter 4

1 James B. Russell, 'Tribute', *SJ,* no. 919NS, January 19, 1892, pp. 443 - 444.

2 H. A. L. Fisher, *James Bryce,* Vol. 1 (London, 1927), p. 25.

3 David Murray, *Memories of the Old College of Glasgow* (Glasgow, 1927), p. 242.

4 Russell, 'Tribute'.

5 Murray, *Memories,* p. 167. However, the obstetric case reported by Christie was under the care of Dr William Leishman. The account was published in *GMJ,* 7, 1860, pp. 471 - 2. I am grateful to Mark Skippen, of the History

of Medicine Centre at Glasgow University, for providing me with this information.

6 Jonathan Andrews and Iain Smith, eds., *Let There Be Light Again; a history of Gartnavel Royal Hospital from its beginnings to the present day* (Glasgow, 1993), p. 65.

7 Andrews and Smith, *Light,* pp. 32 - 3.

8 Andrews and Smith, *Light,* pp. 54, 58, 65.

9 Andrews and Smith, *Light,* p. 61.

10 'House Surgeon's notes for Physician', NHS Greater Glasgow and Clyde Board Archive, HB 13/5/56 pp. 4 - 5, 50, 0.

11 Report for 1862, Gartnavel annual reports, 1861 - 70, NHS Greater Glasgow and Clyde Board Archive, HB 13B 2/219, p. 16.

12 Report for 1863, Gartnavel annual reports, 1861 - 70, NHS Greater Glasgow and Clyde Board Archive, HB 13B 2/219, p. 14.

13 Gartnavel report for 1863, p. 30.

14 JC, 'On Suicidal Impulse', *GMJ*, vol. X11, no. 47, October 1864, pp. 276 - 300.

15 JC, 'Visit to the Convalescent Hospitals of Vincennes and Vesinet, near Paris', April 3, 1865. The undated cutting from the *Glasgow Herald* has been preserved along with Christie's letters to his brother.

Chapter 5

1 Tim Jeal, *Livingstone* (London, 1973), pp. 163 - 4.

2 Jeal, *Livingstone,* p. 224.

3 David Murray, *Memories of the Old College of Glasgow* (Glasgow, 1927), p. 312.

4 Jeal, *Livingstone,* p. 278.

5 Jeal, *Livingstone,* p. 224.

6 A.D.Roberts, 'David Livingstone' in *Dictionary of National Biography* 2000 edition, vol.34, pp. 81 - 2; Jeal, *Livingstone*, pp. 185 - 190.

7 Reginald Coupland, *Livingstone's Last Journey* (London, 1945), p. 13.

8 Jeal, *Livingstone*, p. 235.

9 Bishop Tozer to the Bishop of Cape Town, 6 Jan. 1864 in Gertrude Ward, ed., *Letters of Bishop Tozer and his sister together with some other records of the Universities Mission to Central Africa* (London, 1902), Project Canterbury online edition.

10 Tozer to Bishop, January 6, 1864.

11 Bridglal Pachai, 'The Zambezi Expedition 1858 - 1864: New Highways for Old' in Pachai, ed., *Livingstone, Man of Africa, Memorial Essays, 1873 - 1973* (London, 1973), p.56. See also Coupland, *Livingstone's Last Journey*, p. 32. Coupland records that in a private letter to Horace Waller, a lay member of the mission, Livingstone described Tozer as 'holding fast to his crozier and swathed in his muslins'.

12 David Livingstone to Agnes Livingstone, Mozambique, February 25, 1864, in J.P.R. Wallis, ed., *The Zambezi Expedition of David Livingstone, 1858 - 1863*, vol. 2, p. 382.

13 Tozer to the Rev. J.W. Festing, June 18, 1864 in Ward, *Letters*.

14 Tozer to Miss Tozer, September 1, 1864, in Ward, *Letters*.

15 Quoted in David Livingstone to Agnes Livingstone, Mozambique, February 25, 1864, in Wallis, ed., *Zambesi Expedition*, vol. 2, p. 382.

16 JC to AC, August 22, 1865. Copies of letters from Zanzibar, etc., 1865 - 73, unpublished, Cambridge University Library, Add MS.8163. (All the letters are to Christie's brother Andrew.)

Chapter 6

1 JC to AC, January 4, 1866. Copies of letters from Zanzibar, etc., 1865 - 73, unpublished, Cambridge University Library, Add MS.8163.

2 JC, *Cholera Epidemics in East Africa* (London, 1876), p. 270.

3 Mission to Central Africa: report for parochial use (London, 1865), UMCA box list, A1 (1) B8, Rhodes House archives, Oxford, pp. 18 - 20.

4 JC to AC, January 18, 1866.

5 Editor's introduction, Abdul Sheriff, ed., *The History and Conservation of Zanzibar Stone Town* (Zanzibar Department of Archives, Museums, & Antiquities), p. 1.

6 Jeremy Prestholdt, 'On the Global Repercussions of East African Consumerism', *American Historical Review* vol. 109, no. 3, June 2004. Presthold explains the important role that this trade with Zanzibar played in the industrialisation of Salem, Massachusetts.

7 R. Coupland, *The Exploitation of East Africa, 1856 - 90* (London, 1939), pp. 142 - 3.

8 Coupland, *Exploitation,* pp. 4 - 6.

9 Prestholdt, 'Global Repercussions'. See also Norman R. Bennett, 'Americans in Zanzibar, 1865 - 1915' in Norman R. Bennett (ed.), *Studies on East African History* (Boston, 1963), pp. 31 - 53.

10 J.S. Mangat, *A History of the Asians in East Africa* (Oxford, 1969), pp. 5 - 11. Mangate, who quotes Christie's references to the importance of Indian merchants in Zanzibar, analyses the role of the Bombay government.

11 JC, *Cholera,* pp. 348 - 9.

12 JC, *Cholera,* pp. 324 - 5.

13 JC to AC, March 28, 1866.

14 JC to AC, January 18, 1866.

15 JC, *Cholera*, p. 274.

16 JC, *Cholera*, p. 298.

17 JC, *Cholera*, pp. 272 - 3.

18 JC, *Cholera*, pp. 289 - 297.

Chapter 7

1 JC, *Cholera Epidemics in East Africa* (London, 1876), p. 275.

2 JC to AC, June 4, 1866. Copies of letters from Zanzibar, etc., 1865 – 73, unpublished, Cambridge University Library, Add MS.8163.

3 JC to AC, March 28, 1866.

4 Tim Jeal, *Livingstone* (London, 1973), p. 299.

5 JC to AC, January 18, 1866.

6 JC to AC, June 4, 1866.

7 JC to Mohammed, Kilmarnock, November, 1875, Zanzibar State Archives, ARC4/30. (Mohammed's full name is not given.)

8 JC to AC, January 18, 1866.

9 JC, *Cholera*, pp. 17 – 18.

10 Reginald Coupland, *The Exploitation of East Africa, 1856 – 90* (London, 1939), p. 14.

11 Coupland, *Exploitation*, pp. 18 – 20.

12 Coupland, *Exploitation*, pp. 23 – 4. C. E. B. Russell, *General Rigby, Zanzibar and the Slave Trade* (London, 1935), pp. 115 – 7.

13 Coupland, *Exploitation*, pp. 36 – 7.

14 Coupland, *Exploitation*, pp. 45 – 8. Brown, Yolande, *Zanzibar: May Allen and the Zanzibar Slave Trade* (Shropshire, 2005), p. 90.

15 JC to AC, October 2, 1867.

16 JC to AC, August 20, 1866 and September 18, 1866.

17 JC to AC, April 1, 1867.

Chapter 8

1 Capt. H. A. Fraser to Col. Playfair, British Consul, March 30, 1865, ZSA, AA2/5.

2 Reginald Coupland, *Livingstone's Last Journey* (London, 1945), p. 151.

3 Draft letter from Frere to Granville, 26 March 1873, Sir Bartle Freer's Letter Book, letter no. 38, Zanzibar State Archives AA1/10. Henry M. Stanley, *How I Found Livingstone* (London, 1872), p. 18.

4 David Livingstone to J. Young, November 10, 1866 in Timothy Holmes, ed., *David Livingstone: Letters and Documents, 1841 – 1872* (the Zambian Collection at the Livingstone Museum, Zambia), (Bloomington, 1990) letter 77, p. 114.

5 Fraser to Dr Edward Seward, acting British Consul, March 24, 1866, Zanzibar State Archives, AA2/5. Seward to Fraser, March 24, 1866, Zanzibar State Archives, AA3/22.

6 J. Forbes Munro, *Maritime Enterprise and Empire: Sir William Mackinnon and his business network, 1823-93* (Woodbridge, Suffolk, 2003) pp. 44 and 103.

7 Munro, *Maritime Enterprise*, p. 85n.

8 Munro, *Maritime Enterprise*, p. 84.

9 Reginald Coupland, *The Exploitation of East Africa, 1856 – 1890* (London, 1939), p. 178.

10 Edward Steere, 'Central African Mission: its present state and prospects (1873)', p. 23, Rhodes House Library, Oxford, Universities Mission to Central Africa box list A1 (II) A. The high mortality rate of the UMCA is discussed by Michael Jennings in 'The Mysterious and Intangible Enemy: Health and Disease among the Early UMCA Missionaries, 1860 – 1918' in *Social History of Medicine*

vol. 15 no.1, pp.65 – 87. Jennings claims that the mission, which was badly under-resourced, lacked any form of disease-management strategy, leaving responsibility for health with the individual. He does not mention Christie's role as honorary physician. The mission's mortality rate remained high – averaging 17.5 per cent – until the mid-1890s.

11 John Kirk to unnamed correspondent, July 28, 1866. National Library of Scotland, Acc. 9942/4.

12 JC to AC, April 1, 1867. Copies of letters from Zanzibar, etc., 1865 – 73, unpublished, Cambridge University Library, Add MS.8163.

13 J. Forbes Munro, 'Shipping subsidies and railway guarantees: William Mackinnon, Eastern Africa and the Indian Ocean, 1860-93' in *The Journal of African History* vol. 28 (1987), p. 215.

14 Coupland, *Exploitation,* p. 178.

15 David Livingstone to W.C. Oswell, March 21, 1865 in Holmes, ed., *Livingstone: Letters,* letter 77, p.114.

16 Coupland, *Exploitation,* p. 179.

17 Fraser to Seward, February 15, 1867, ZSA, AA2/5. Norman B. Bedingfeld, Captain, HMS *Wasp* to Seward, March 4, 1867, Z SA, AA1/13.

18 Foreign Office to Playfair, June 1, 1867, ZSA, AA1/7.

19 Lord Stanley to Seward, June 14, 1867, ZSA, AA1/7.

20 Fraser to Foreign Office, August 14, 1867, ZSA, AA1/7. Lawyers to F.O., October 22, 1867, Z SA, AA1/7. F O to Fraser, December 19, 1867, ZSA, AA1/7.

21 JC to H.A. Churchill, British Consul, December 28, 1867, ZSA, AA2/6.

22 JC to AC, April 1, 1867.

23 JC to AC, August 20, 1868 and July 29, 1869.

Chapter 9

1 JC to AC, January 24, 1869. Copies of letters from Zanzibar, etc., 1865 – 73, unpublished, Cambridge University Library, Add MS.8163.

2 JC to AC, January. 24, 1869.

3 JC to AC, April 16, 1869.

4 JC to AC, May 29, 1869.

5 David Livingstone to W.C. Oswell, September 29, 1865 in Timothy Holmes, ed., *David Livingstone: Letters and Documents, 1841 – 1872; the Zambian Collection at the Livingstone Museum* (Zambia), (Bloomington, 1990),p.151. Livingstone to James Young, January 26, 1866 in William Garden Blaikie, *Personal Life of David Livingstone* (London, 1925), pp. 308 – 9. Reginald Coupland, *The Exploitation of East Africa, 1856-1890* (London: Faber and Faber, 1939), pp. 39-40.

6 JC to AC, May 29, 1869.

7 JC to AC, September 9, 1867.

8 JC to AC, January 24, 1869.

9 Robert Kidd might not have occupied this post until a little later. The exact date of his appointment by the Earl of Dalhousie, owner of the castle, is unknown although it was certainly before 1879.

10 JC to AC, July 29, 1869.

11 Otway, Foreign Office to Churchill, July 5,1870; Tozer to Clarendon (Foreign Secretary), April 8, 1870; Foreign Office to Tozer, July 4, 1870: ZSA AA1/7.

Chapter 10

1 JC, *Cholera Epidemics in East Africa* (London, 1876), pp. 361 – 2.

2 Kirk to Governor of Bengal, November 25, 1869, British consular correspondence, outward, ZSA.

Notes

3 JC, *Cholera*, p. 365.

4 JC, *Cholera*, pp. 367 – 8.

5 JC, *Cholera*, pp. 377 – 80.

6 JC to AC, February 7, 1870. Copies of letters from Zanzibar, etc., 1865 – 73, unpublished, Cambridge University Library, Add MS.8163. Christie, *Cholera*, pp. 382 – 4.

7 JC, *Cholera*, p. 389 – 90.

8 JC, *Cholera*, p. 387.

9 JC, *Cholera*, pp. 399 – 402.

10 JC, *Choler*, pp. 405 – 9.

11 JC, *Cholera*, pp. 409 – 10.

12 JC, *Cholera*, pp. 402 – 4.

13 JC, *Cholera*, p. 390.

14 Alain Contrepois, 'The clinician, germs and infectious diseases: the example of Charles Bouchard in Paris', *Medical History* vol. 46 (2002), p. 197. Early experiments in the use of carbolic acid for the treatment of cholera are discussed in Arthur Ernest Sanson, *The Arrest and Prevention of Cholera: being a Guide to the Antiseptic Treatment with New Observations on Causation* (London, 1866). Sanson commented that although the reports from the Belle Isle Hospital, where the treatment had been tried, were still *sub judice*, it appeared that 'the carbolic acid system had been most successful.' More common treatments were calomel, given to restore liver function, and opium. Quinine, strychnine, arsenic, sulphur and sulphuric acid were among the many other drugs administered. Emetics, bleeding and hot baths were also tried. See Harold Scott, *A History of Tropical Medicine* (London, 1939), vol. 2, p. 685. Scott remarks that the variety of nineteenth-century treatments illustrates the truth of the saying that 'a disease with many remedies has no cure.' The use of saline infusions throughout the nineteenth century is discussed in Norman Howard-Jones, 'Cholera therapy in the nineteenth century',

Journal of the History of Medicine (October 1972), pp. 389 – 92.Though this was eventually to become the standard treatment for cholera Howard-Jones attributes its failure in the nineteenth century to imperfect equipment and lack of aseptic precautions.

15 JC, *Cholera*, p. 495. See Howard-Jones, 'Cholera therapy', p. 384. Iwan Rhys Morus, 'The Measure of Man: technologizing the Victorian Body', *History of Science*, vol. 37, no. 117 (September 1999), pp. 249 – 77. In his account of the proliferation of medical applications of electricity in the second half of the nineteenth century the author states that by the general hospitals were opening electrical departments. The development of the various forms of electrical treatment administered is described by Rhys Morus in 'Marketing the Machine: the Construction of Electrotherapeutics as Viable Medicine in Victorian England', *Medical History*, vol. 36 (January, 1999), pp. 37 ff.

16 Howard-Jones, 'Cholera therapy', p. 376.

17 JC, *Cholera*, pp. 402, 411 – 13.

18 JC, *Cholera*, pp. 415 – 6.

19 JC 'Notes on the cholera epidemics in East Africa', *The Lancet,* January 28, 1871, pp. 113 – 115; Christie, *Cholera*, p.416.

20 JC to AC, February 7, 1870.

21 JC, *Cholera*, p.495.

22 Daniel Liebowitz, *The Physician and the Slave Trade: John Kirk, the Livingstone Expedition, and the Crusade against Slavery in East Africa* (New York, 1998), pp. 151 – 2.

Chapter 11

1 JC, *Cholera Epidemics in East Africa* (London, 1876), pp. 417 – 8.

2 JC, *Cholera*, pp. 394 – 6.

3 JC, *Cholera*, pp. 418 – 9. See also Kirk's annual report, July 1870, Papers of John Kirk, NLS, Acc. 9942/6.

4 JC, *Cholera*, pp. 489 – 90.

5 JC, *Cholera*, pp. 490 – 1.

6 JC, *Cholera*, pp. 492 – 3.

7 JC, *Cholera*, pp. 405 – 6.

8 JC, 'On Epidemics of Dengue Fever: Their Diffusion and Etiology' in *GMJ*, vol. 16, no. 3, September, 1881, pp.161 – 176.

9 JC, 'Notes on the cholera epidemics in East Africa', *The Lancet*, January 28, 1871, pp. 113 – 15.

10 JC to AC, June 10, 1871. Copies of letters from Zanzibar, etc., 1865 – 73, unpublished, Cambridge University Library, Add MS.8163.

11 JC, *Cholera*, Preface, p. x.

12 JC, *Cholera*, Preface, p. xiii.

13 JC, *Cholera*, p. 101.

14 JC, *Cholera*, pp. 140 – 1 ; Christie to AC, June 4, 1866.

15 JC, *Cholera*, pp. 118 – 9, 146 – 7.

16 JC, *Cholera*, pp.153-164. The bizarre Abyssinian expedition forms the plot of one George Macdonald Fraser's 'Flashman' novels, *Flashman on the March* (London, 2005).

17 JC, *Cholera*, pp.165 – 8, 187.

18 JC, *Cholera*, pp. 192 – 3.

19 JC, *Cholera*, pp. 229 – 234.

20 Mark Harrison, 'Public Health in British India', *Cambridge History of Medicine* (ed Charles Webster and Charles Rosenberg), (Cambridge, 1994), pp. 100, 105 – 7.

21 Harrison, *Public Health*, pp. 100 – 2.

Chapter 12

1 J. Forbes Munro, 'Shipping subsidies and railway guarantees: William Mackinnon, Eastern Africa and the Indian Ocean', *Journal of African History* 28 (1987), pp 209-30; George Blake, *British India Centenary, 1856-1956* (London, 1956), p.146.

2 JC to AC, February 4, 1871. Copies of letters from Zanzibar, etc, 1865 – 73, unpublished, Cambridge University Library, Add MS.8163.

3 JC to AC, June 10, 1871. The Admiral died only a few months later.

4 JC to AC, March 14, 1873, May 12, 1873.

5 JC to AC, July 12, 1870, November 13, 1871.

6 JC to AC, April 20, 1872; May 30, 1872; Miss Tozer to the editor of the *Guardian*, Zanzibar, April 18, 1872; 'Terrible cyclone at Zanzibar, from a special report to the *Times of India*, *North Otago Times* July 26, 1872, p. 3 .

7 JC to AC, May 30, 1872.

8 Anthony Preston and John Major, *Send a Gunboat! A study of the gunboat and its role in British policy, 1854 – 1904* (London, 1967), p. 130; Reginald Coupland, *The Exploitation of East Africa* (London, 1939), pp. 161 – 3; William Cope Devereux, *A Cruise in the Gorgon* (London, 1869), pp. 88 – 9. Devereux, who was paymaster of HMS *Gorgon*, describes a boarding.

9 JC to AC, August 20, 1866.

10 JC to AC, 18 September 1866, 20 August 1866.

11 Norman R. Bennett, *Studies in East African History* (Boston, 1963), pp. 31 – 40. Bennett, in his study of Americans in Zanzibar, notes that the opening of the Suez Canal was a setback for American traders because it brought Europe nearer to Zanzibar.

12 Foreign Office to Kirk, October 22, 1869; November 5, 1869; November 16, 1869; and February 25, 1870, ZSA, AA1/7, inward letters, 1869 and 1870; extract from report

of the Register of the High Court of Admiralty, August 23, 1869, ZSA, AA1/7, inward letters, 1869.

13 Captain H.A. Fraser, the Rt. Rev. Bishop Tozer and James Christie, MD, *East African Slave Trade, Measures Proposed for its Extinction as Viewed by Residents in Zanzibar* (London, 1871).

14 JC to AC, November 13, 1871.

15 Draft letter to Granville, Foreign Secretary, January 14, 1873 in 'Sir Bartle Frere's letterbook on his mission to Zanzibar: draft letters outward from the time of his appointment to the end of his mission in Muscat', ZSA, AA1/10, letter no. 8, pp. 117 – 8.

16 JC to AC, December 18, 1872 and January 4, 1873.

17 Draft letter to Granville, February 10, 1873 in 'Sir Bartle Frere's letterbook', ZSA, AA1/10, letter 15. John Webb's views are discussed in Peter Duignan and Lewis H. Gann, *The United States and Africa* (Cambridge, 1984), p. 142.

18 Draft letters to Granville, 'Sir Bartle Frere's letterbook', Zanzibar State Archives, AA1/10, nos. 35 and 8; Lord Lytton, British Ambassador in Paris, to Granville, enclosed by Enfield, Foreign Office in letter to Kirk, April 24, 1873, ZSA, AA1/11.

19 Draft letter to Granville in 'Sir Bartle Frere's letterbook', March 26, 1873, ZSA, AA1/10, letter no. 38.

20 Draft letter to Granville in 'Sir Bartle Frere's letterbook', March 26, 1873, ZSA, AA1/10, letter no. 38.

21 Granville to Kirk, May 9, 1873, ZSA AA1/11.

Chapter 13

1 JC to AC, November 9, 1867, August 25, 1868. Copies of letters from Zanzibar, etc., 1865 – 73, unpublished, Cambridge University Library, Add MS.8163.

2 Henry M. Stanley, *How I found Livingstone: Travels, Adventures, and Discoveries in Central Africa* (London,

1872), pp. 14 – 15. See also Tim Jeal, *Stanley: The Impossible Life of Africa's Greatest Explorer* (London, 2007), p. 95. Francis Webb, described by Stanley as a pleasant cynic, stood to gain from a successful mission by Stanley. James L. Newman, in *Imperial Footprints: Henry Morton Stanley's African Journals* (London, 2004) points out that this would have re-energised American interest in Zanzibar and profited Webb's firm, John Bertram and Co., of Salem, Massachusetts.

3 JC to AC, February 4, 1871.

4 Stanley, *Livingstone*, pp. 67 – 8.

5 Letter from H.M. Stanley to JC, from Quihara, Myanembe, August 14, 1871, and later undated letter from Stanley to J C, in 'Letters from H M Stanley to Dr Christie', uncatalogued archives at the David Livingstone Centre, Blantyre, Accession no. 784. See also Ian Anstruther, *Stanley's Triumph and Disaster* (London, 1956), pp. 69 – 70, footnote p. 197.

6 JC to AC, June 10, 1871; Stanley, *Livingstone*, p. 662.

7 Stanley, *Livingstone*, p. 662.

8 Stanley, *Livingstone*, pp. 13-14.

9 Jeal, *Stanley*, p. 135.

10 Reginald Coupland, *Livingstone's Last Journey* (London, 1945), pp. 199 – 200.

11 JC to AC, January 4, 1873.

12 JC to AC, December 18, 1872.

13 The *Natal Colonist*, June 5, 1874. The cutting was preserved along with Christie's letters to his brother.

14 'The Bones of the Matter: The Identification of the remains of David Livingstone' in *Treasures of the College* (celebrating 300 years of the library of the Royal College of Physicians and Surgeons of Glasgow), ed. James J. Beaton, Roy Miller and Iain T. Boyle (Glasgow 1998) p.176.

Notes

15 Miss Tozer to Miss Twining, April 5, 1872 in Gertrude Ward, ed., *Letters of Bishop Tozer and his sister together with some other records of the Universities Mission to Central Africa* (London, 1902), Project Canterbury online edition.

16 Extract from letter from Bishop Tozer to the Bishop of Lincoln, January 17, 1865, Rhodes House Library, Oxford, A1(I)2, p.132.

17 The Zanzibar Diary of John Kirk, 1867 – 75, undated entry, March, 1872 and April 4, 1872, Papers of John Kirk and Helen Kirk, National Library of Scotland, Ms division, 25.

18 Miss Tozer to Miss Twining, August 8, 1872.

19 JC to AC, August 19, 1872.

20 Miss Tozer to Miss Twining, June 23, 1872.

21 JC to AC, January 4, 1873.

22 A newspaper cutting describing the route has been preserved along with Christie's letters.

Chapter 14

1 R.A. Cage, 'Population and Employment Characteristics' in R.A. Cage, ed., *The Working Class in Glasgow, 1750-1914* (London, 1987), pp. 9 – 16.

2 'Tribute by Dr Russell', *SJ* no. 919, NS, January. 19, 1892, pp. 443 – 4.

3 'Obituary: John Netten Radcliffe', *British Medical Journal*, September 20, 1884; 2 (1238), p. 588.

4 JC, *Cholera Epidemics in East Africa* (London, 1876), Preface, pp. xii – xiii.

5 JC, *Cholera*, Preface, p. xiv.

6 Christie, *Cholera*, pp. 454-474.

7 'Tribute by Dr Russell', *SJ*, p. 443.

8 Simon Carvalho and Mark Zacher, 'The International Health Regulations in Historical Perspective' in Andrew T. Price-Smith, ed., *Plagues and Politics: Infectious Disease and International Policy* (New York: 1999), pp. 237 – 8. Valeska Huber, 'The Unification of the globe by disease? The international sanitary conferences on cholera, 1851 – 94' in *The Historical Journal* vol. 49, no. 2 (2006), pp. 458, 464.

9 The reviews are quoted in 'Testimonials in favour of James Christie', 1880, Glasgow University Library, Special Collections RQ 1637.

10 'Tribute by Dr Russell', *SJ* p. 444.

11 Rona Gaffney, 'Poor Law Hospitals, 1845 – 1914' in Olive Checkland and Margaret Lamb, eds, *Health Care as Social History: the Glasgow Case* (Aberdeen, 1982), p. 44.

12 GCA, D HEW 1/5/3 p. 59. I am indebted to Dr David Sutton, of the Centre for the History of Medicine, University of Glasgow, for this reference.

13 M.A. Simpson, *The Pattern of Local Government in the Western Suburbs of Glasgow in the Nineteenth Century*, (unpublished manuscript, Mitchell Library, Glasgow) vol. 2, pp. 3 -6.

14 'James Dobbie, MD: obituary', *GMJ*, April, 1878, pp. 179 – 80.

Chapter 15

1 JC to AC, August 20, 1866.

2 Henry Brougham Morton, *A Hillhead Album* (Glasgow: 1973). (The pages of the album are unnumbered.)

3 J.J. Bell, *I Remember* (Edinburgh: 1932), pp. 144 – 5.

4 Bell, *I Remember*, p. 42.

5 M.A. Simpson, 'Middle-class Housing and the Growth of Suburban Communities in the West End of Glasgow, 1830-1900': unpublished thesis submitted for the degree of Bachelor of Letters of the University of Glasgow, 1970, vol. 1, pp.1 97 – 8.

Notes

6 Burgh of Hillhead, MOH reports, GCA H-Hil 5/5.

7 Burgh of Hillhead, Medical Officer's Report for the year 1886, pp. 3- 5, GCA H-Hil 5/5/1.

8 Burgh of Hillhead, Medical Officer's Report for the year 1890, pp.1 – 4, GCA H-Hil 5/5.

9 Hillhead MO's Report for 1890, p. 5, GCA H-Hil 15/5; Simpson, 'Middle-class Housing,' vol. 1, p. 211.

10 Burgh of Hillhead, Medical Officer's Report on the Infectious Diseases (Notification) Act, 1889, 5 Jun. 1890, GCA H-Hil 15/5.

11 See, for example, Burgh of Hillhead, Special Sanitary Report, 7 Oct. 1887, GCA H-Hil 15/5. Simpson reported that he had been 'directed by Dr Christie' to report on the drainage of tenements in Westbank Quadrant, where the main sewer was too shallow to drain the building.

12 JC, Report to the Local Authority of Barony Parish on an outbreak of fever at Possilpark during the months of April and May, 1880, GCA G.614.511. For Russell's side of the investigation see Glasgow Town Council Health Committee Minutes, October 21, 1889, GCA E.1 20.12, p. 108.

13 JC, 'An Historical Sketch of Sanitary Science' (introductory lecture delivered at Anderson's College, Glasgow, May 19, 1879), *Glasgow Medical Journal*, vol. xii no.x, October, 1879, pp. 241 – 257.

14 T. Brown Henderson, *The History of the Glasgow Dental Hospital and School, 1879-1939* (Glasgow: 1960.). Edna Robertson, 'Public Health and Dentistry: the dog that didn't bite,' *The History of Dentistry Research Group Newsletter*, April 2000.

15 'Obituary: the Late James Christie', *GMJ*, vol. 37, 1892, pp. 126-7

16 The Anderson College professors and lecturers were listed annually in the *Medical Directory*.

17 JC, 'Historical Sketch of Sanitary Science'.

18 JC, 'On Provident Dispensaries as a Means for Promoting the Public Health', read before the Philosophical Society of Glasgow, March 3, 1880 (Glasgow, 1880). The paper is discussed in Thomas Ferguson, *Scottish Social Welfare, 1864- 1914* (Edinburgh and London, 1958), p. 445.

19 JC, 'The Fundamental Principles of Disinfection', an address delivered at the opening of the disinfection station of the Burgh of Hillhead, April 9, 1881 (Glasgow, 1881).

20 JC, 'Sanitation in Small Towns and Rural Districts, *SJ*, No. 170 NS, April 19, 1980, pp. 33-48.

21 Minutes of the Health Committee of Glasgow Police Board, June 14, 1880 and October 4, 1880, GCA E1 20.5, pp. 224, 297.

22 Letters from H.M. Stanley to JC, January 25, 1878 and undated, in 'Letters from H M Stanley to Dr Christie', uncatalogued archive at the David Livingstone Centre, Blantyre, Accession no. 784.

23 Thomas McCall Anderson, *A Treatise on Diseases of the Skin, with Special Reference to their Diagnosis and Treatment: including an analysis of 11,000 consecutive cases* (London, 1887).

24 W.F. Bynum, *Science and the Practice of Medicine in the Nineteenth Century* (Cambridge: 1994), p. 142. Bynum describes the congress as 'special, in both its participation and visibility'.

25 JC, 'On Epidemics of Dengue Fever: their Diffusion and Etiology', *GMJ*, vol. xvi, no. 3, pp. 161 – 176.

26 'Tribute by Dr Russell', *SJ* no. 919, NS, January 19, 1892, pp. 443 – 4

Chapter 16

1 Edna Robertson, *Glasgow's Doctor: James Burn Russell, 1837-1904* (East Linton, 1998), pp.138 – 9.

2 Letter from Matthew Hay, MOH for Aberdeen, dated June 5, 1890, in 'Testimonials in favour of James Christie', GAC H-HIL 15/4 (44).

3 Letters from W.J. Simpson, Professor John G. McKendrick, John C. McVail, Professor Ebeneezer Duncan and Samson Gemmell in 'Testimonials'.

4 M.A. Simpson, 'Middle-class Housing and the Growth of Suburban Communities in the West End of Glasgow, 1830 – 1900', unpublished thesis submitted for the degree of Bachelor of Letters of the University of Glasgow, 1970, vol. 1, p. 166.

5 *Paisley and Renfrewshire Gazette*, October 11, 1890, p. 5. I am grateful to David Weir, Local Studies Librarian, Paisley Central Library, for checking the records.

6 JC to AC, November 21, 1890.

7 'Tribute by Dr Russell', *SJ*, no. 919, NS, Jan. 19, 1892, pp. 443-4.

8 Simpson, 'Middle-class Housing', vol.1, p.172.

Chapter 17

1 *SJ*, 919NS, January 19, 1892, p. 440.

2 'Tribute by Dr Russell', *SJ*, 919 NS, January 19, 1892, p. 444.

3 *The Lancet*, January 16, 1892, p. 17.

4 Anna Crozier, *The Colonial Medical Service in British East Africa* (London, 2007), p. 7.

Christie of Zanzibar

INDEX

Index